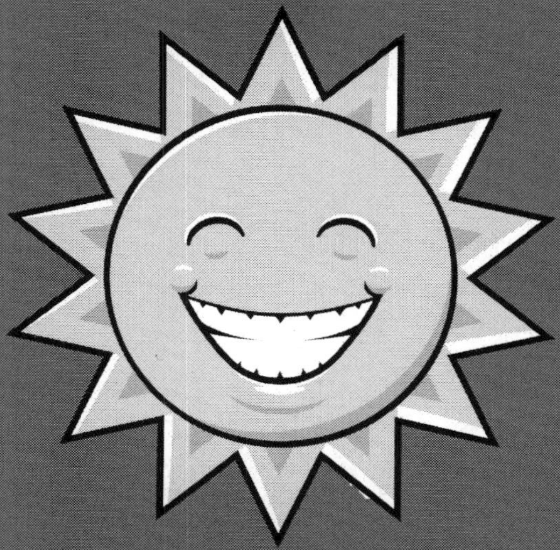

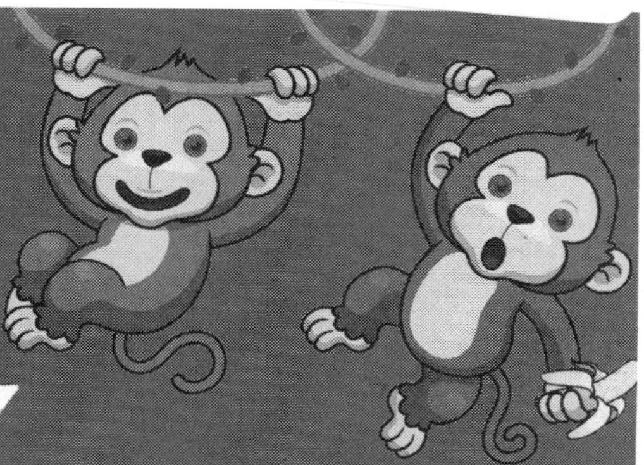

MY FIRST COLORING BOOK

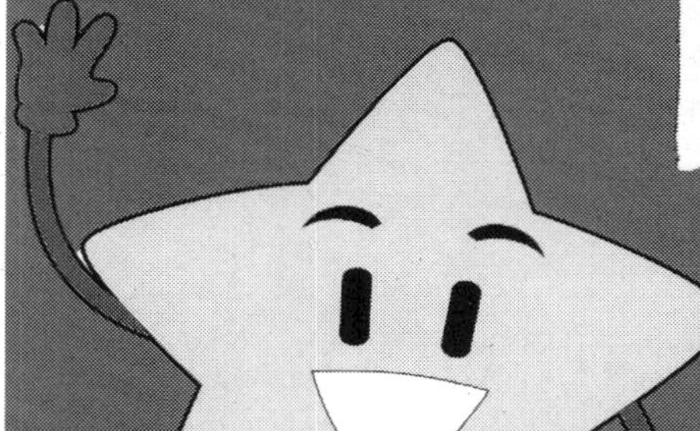

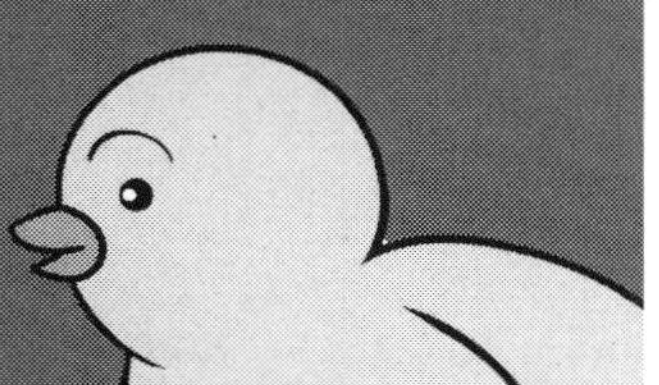

Cleo S. Baker

MY FIRST COLORING BOOK

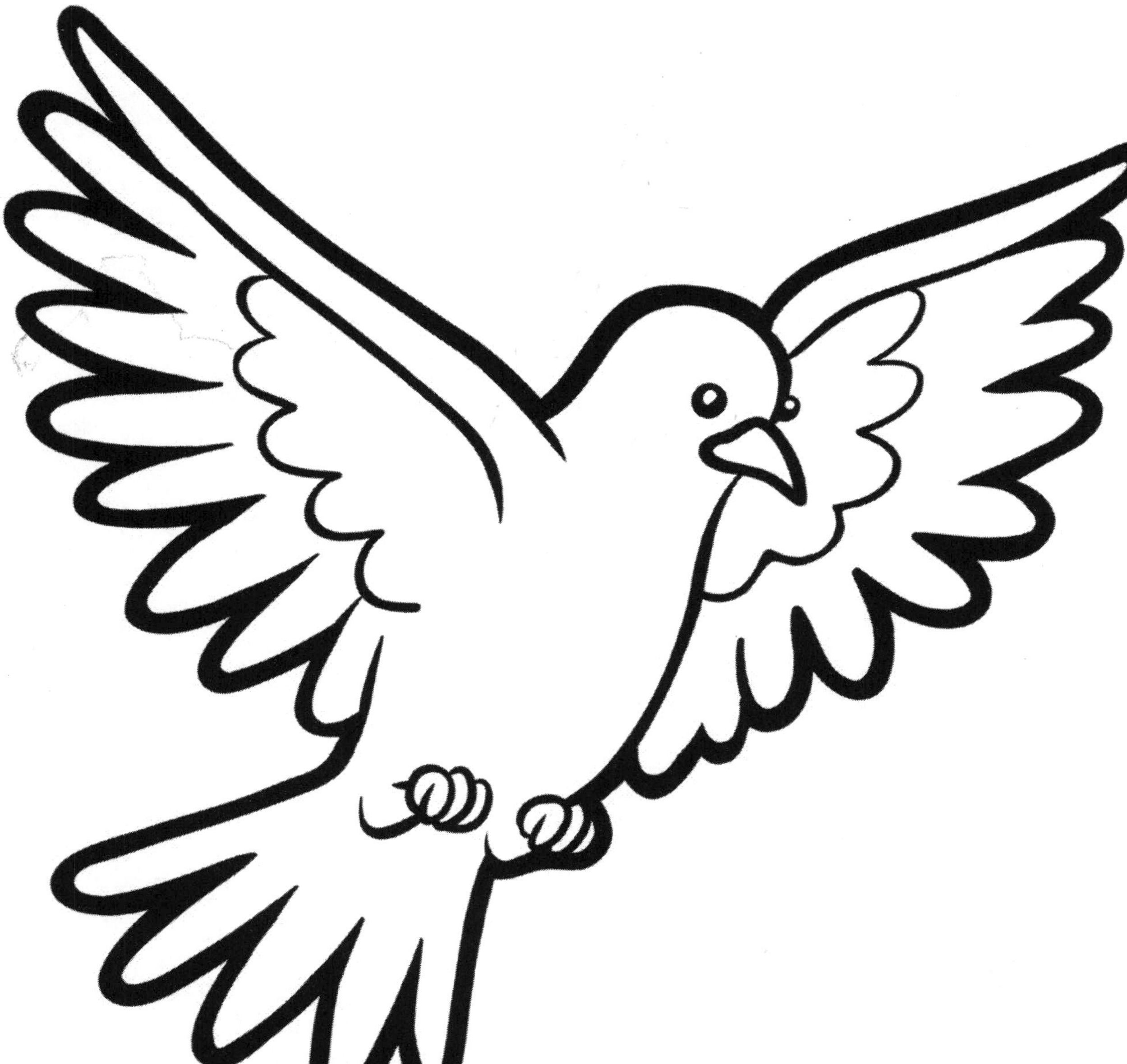

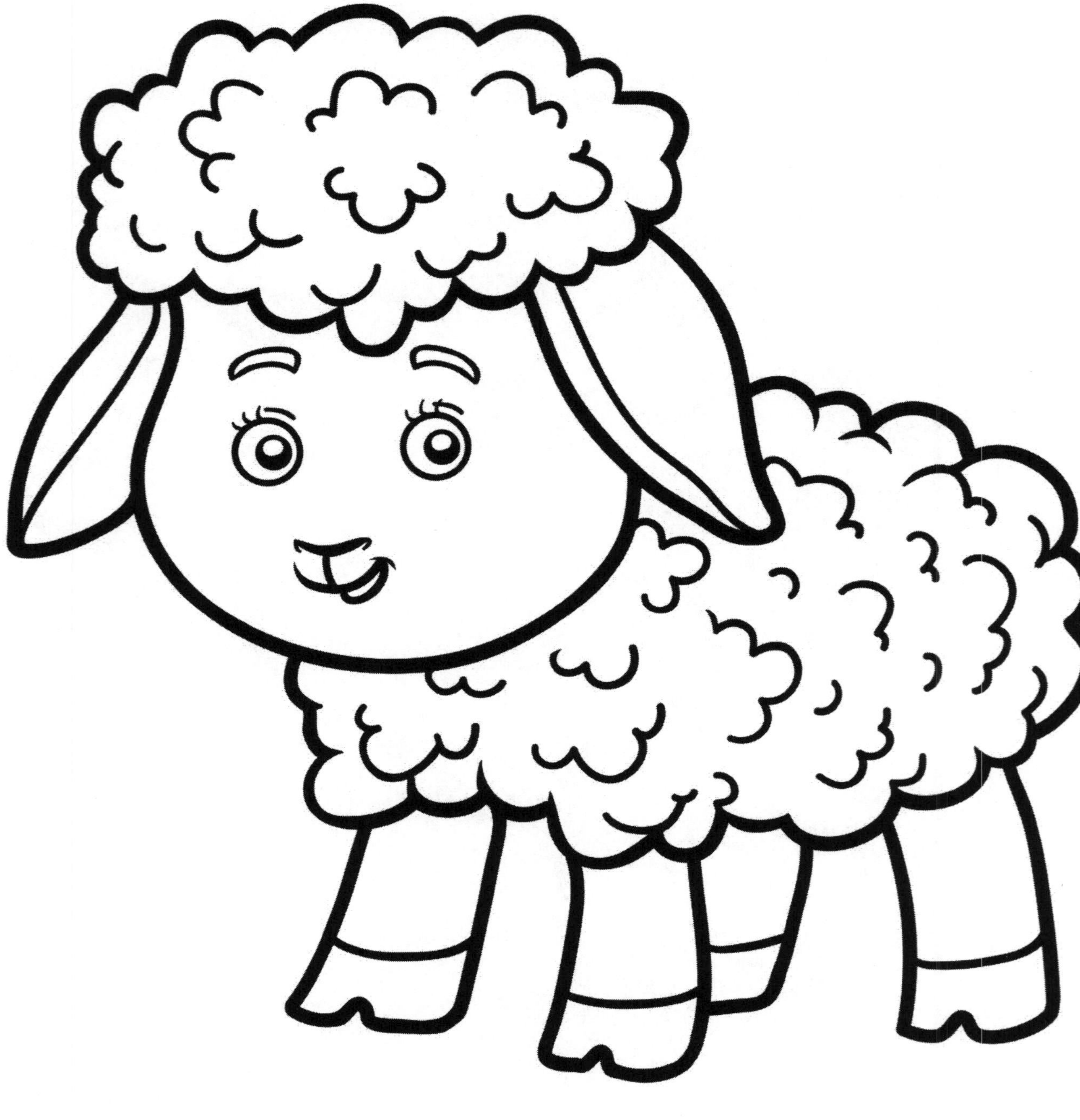

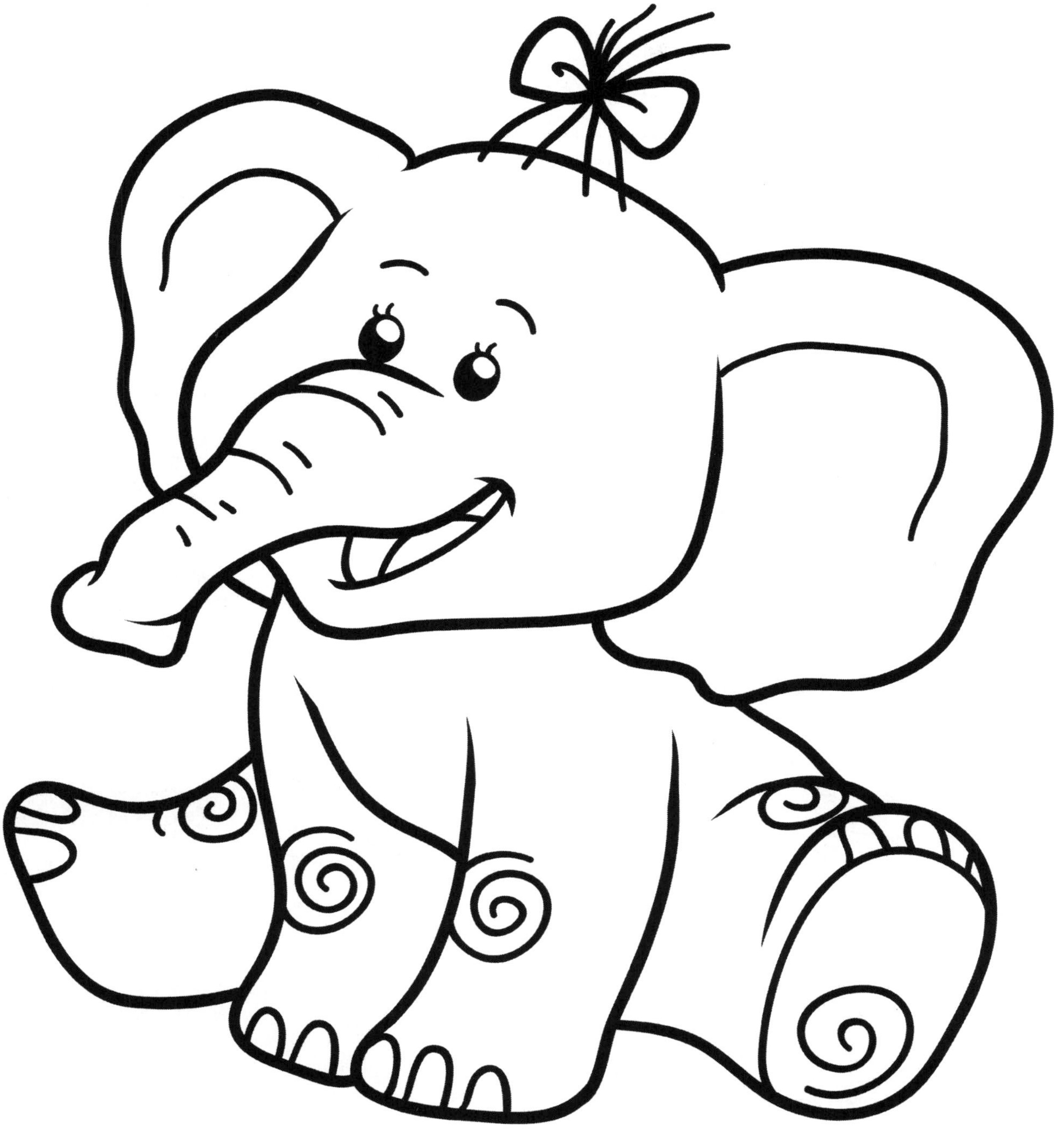

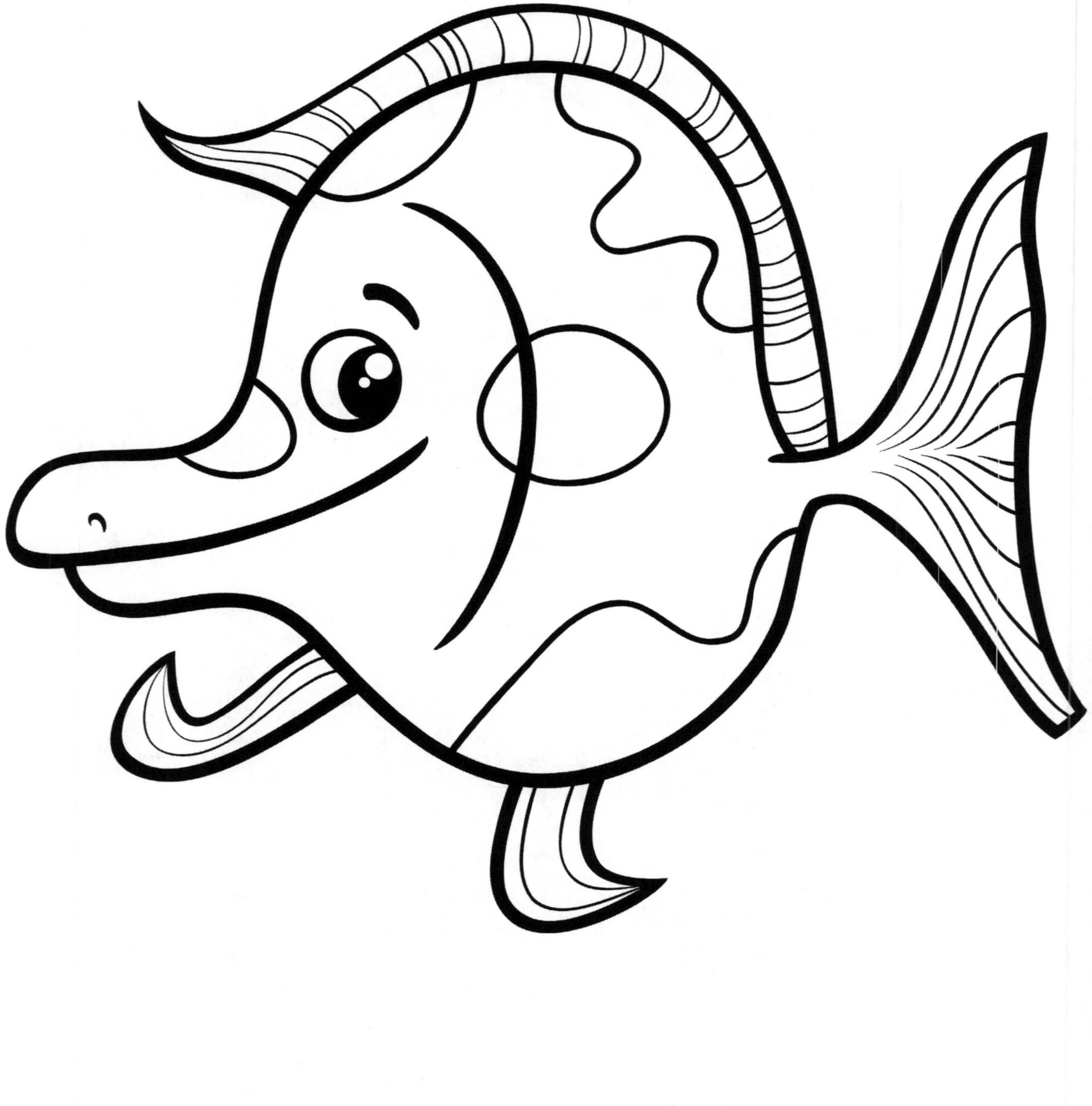

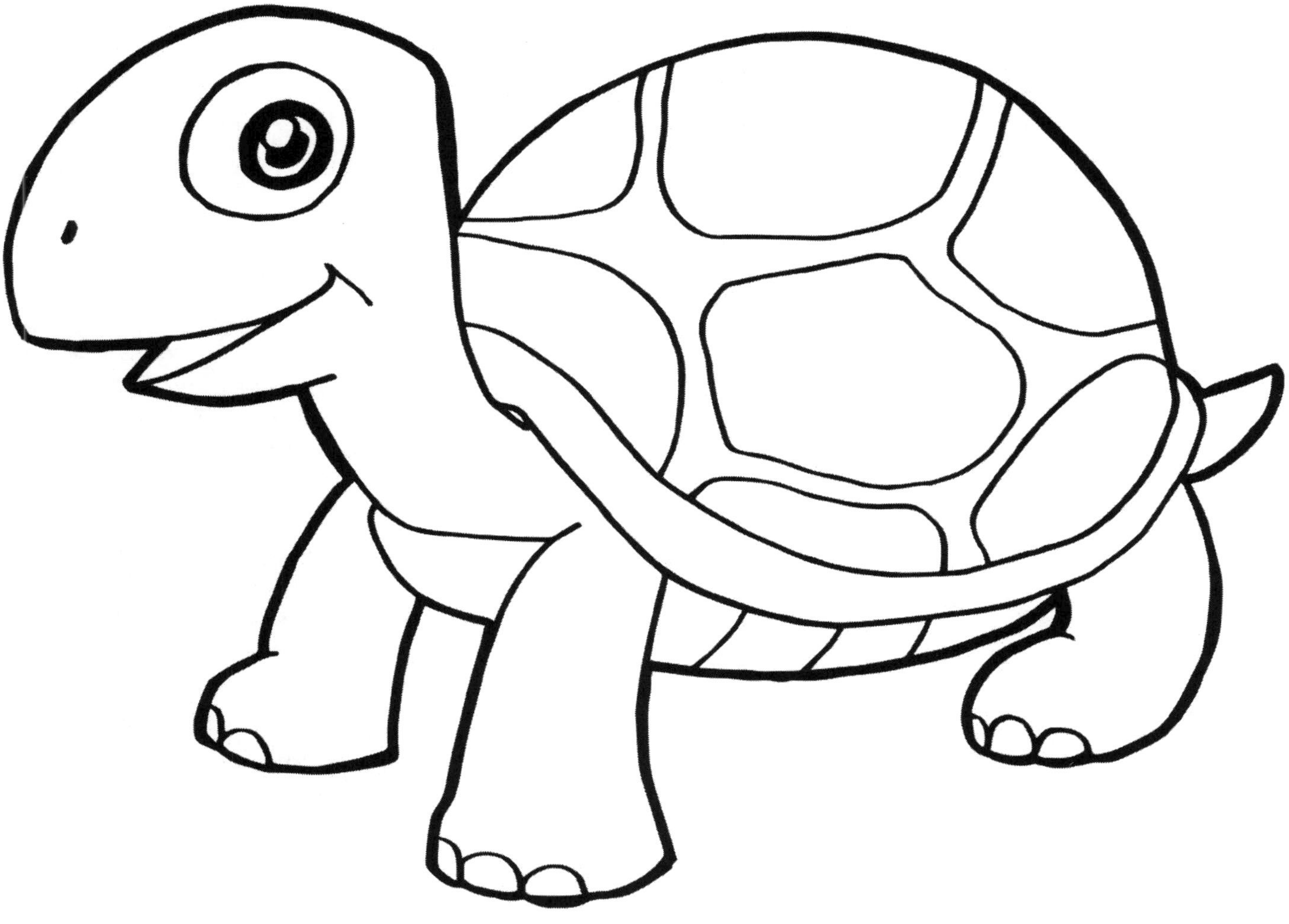

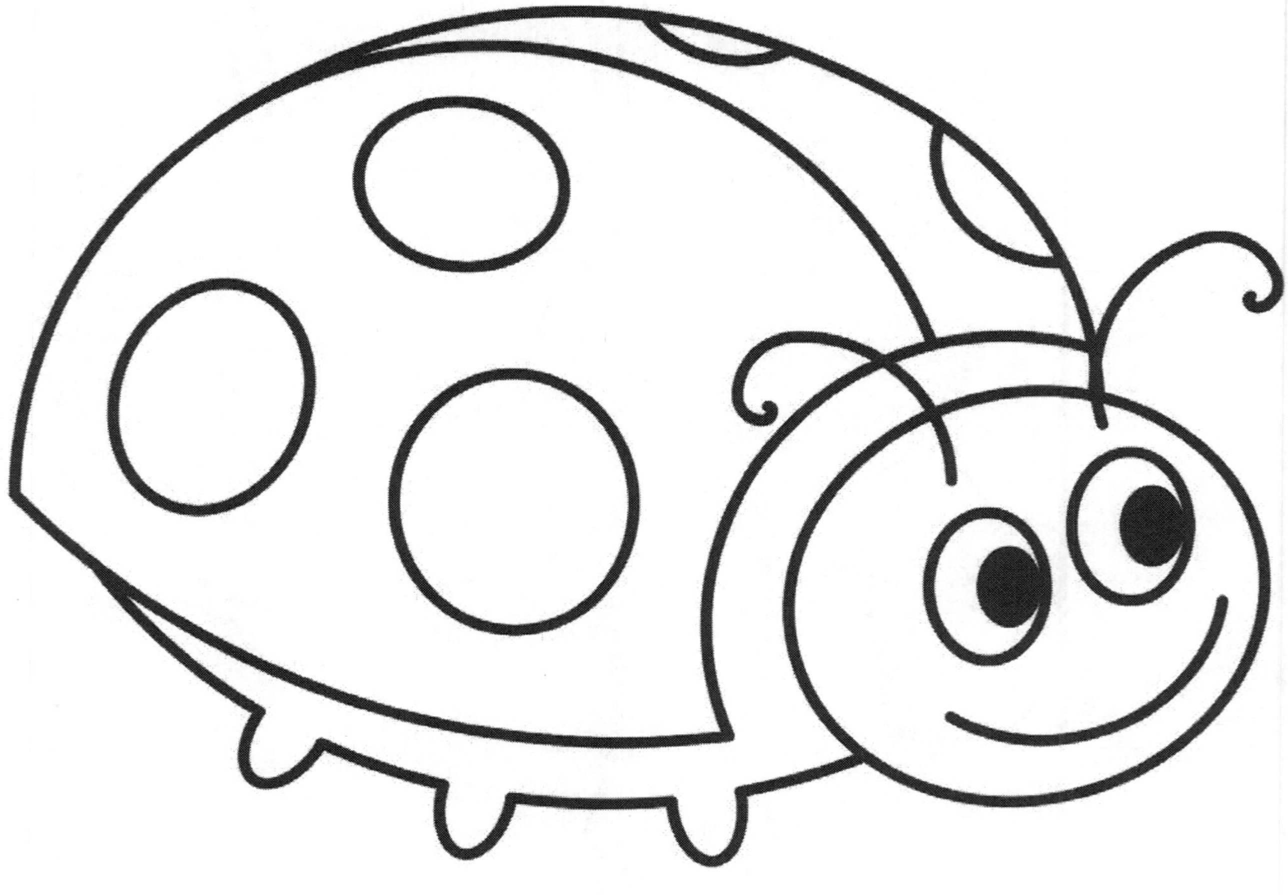

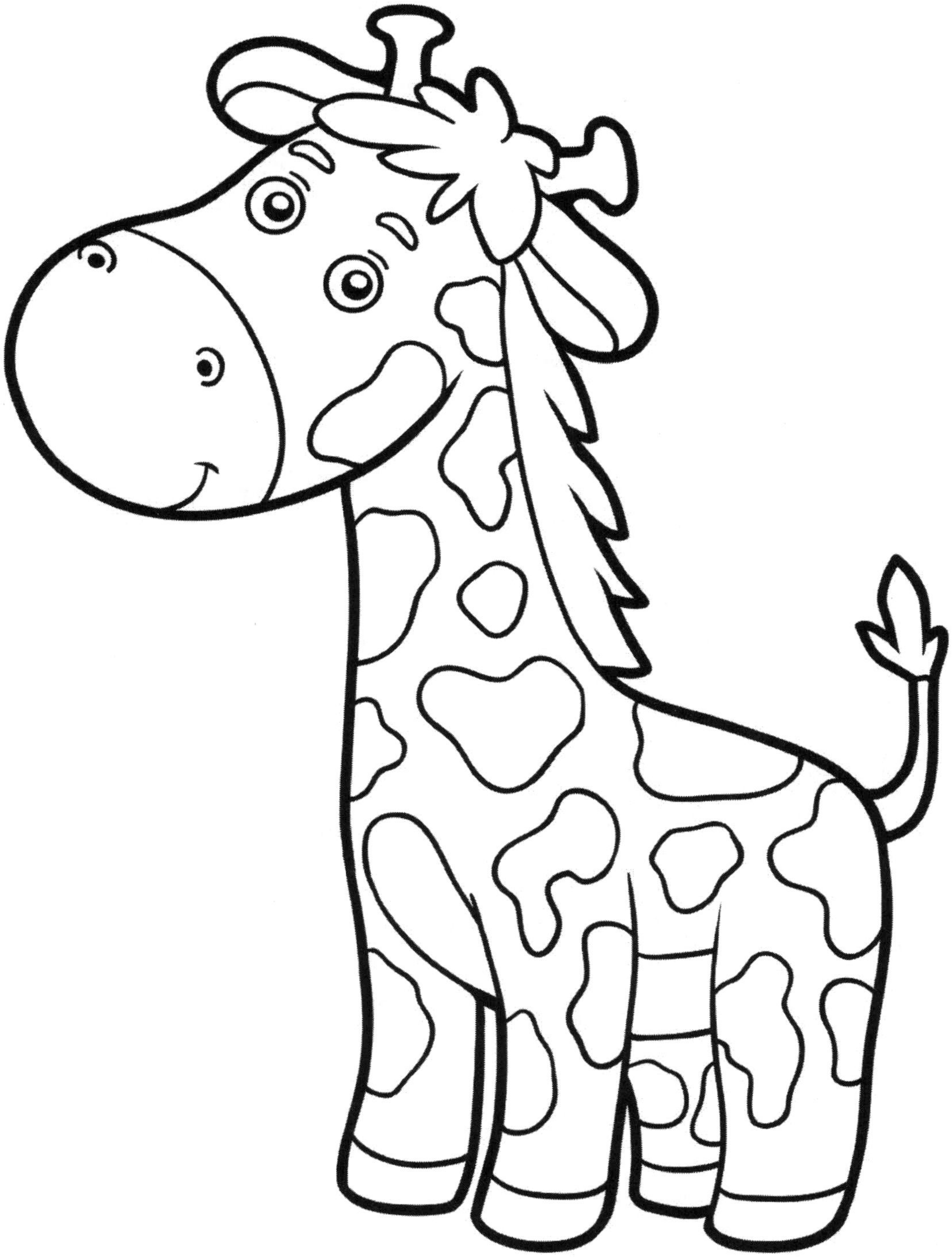

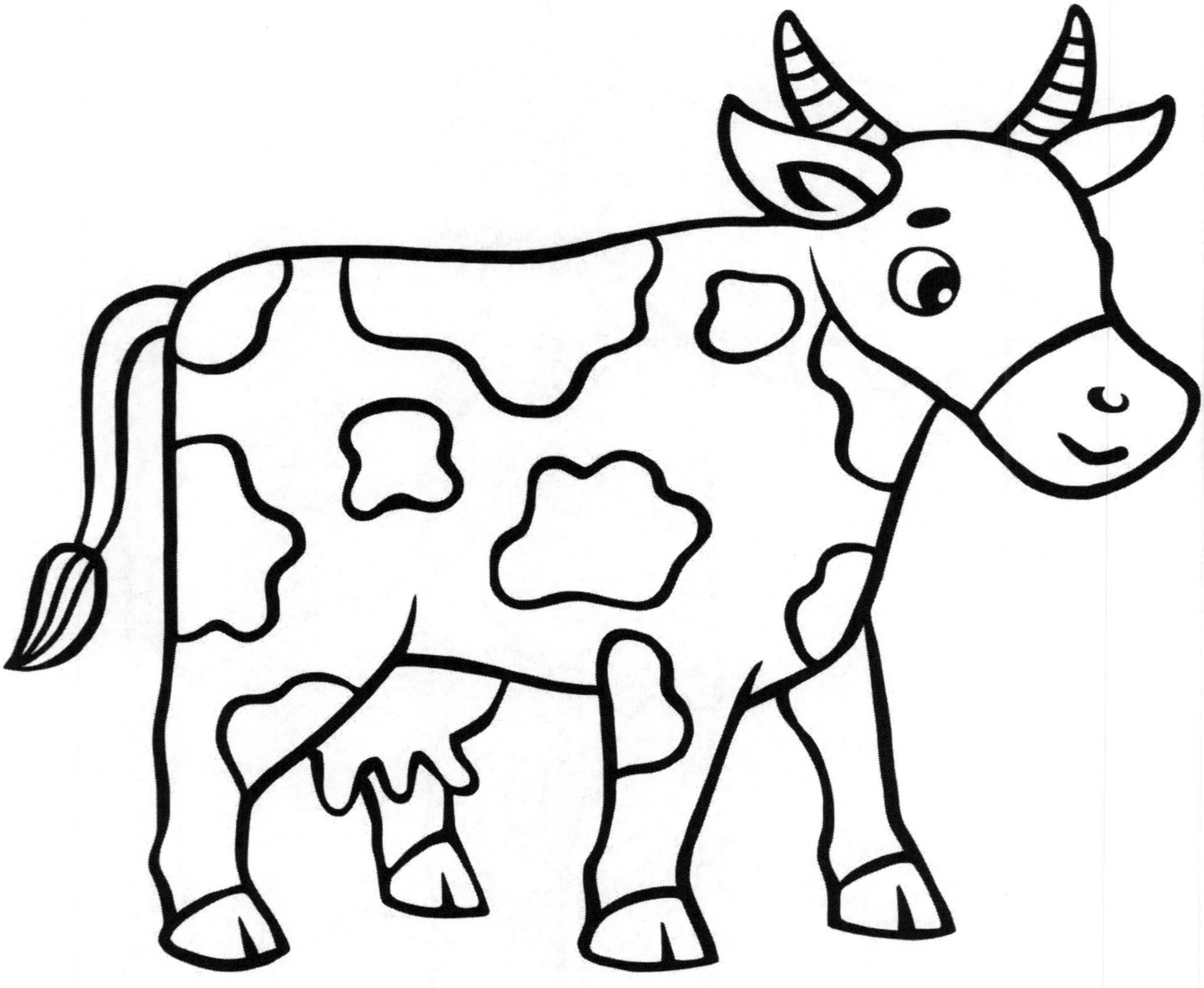

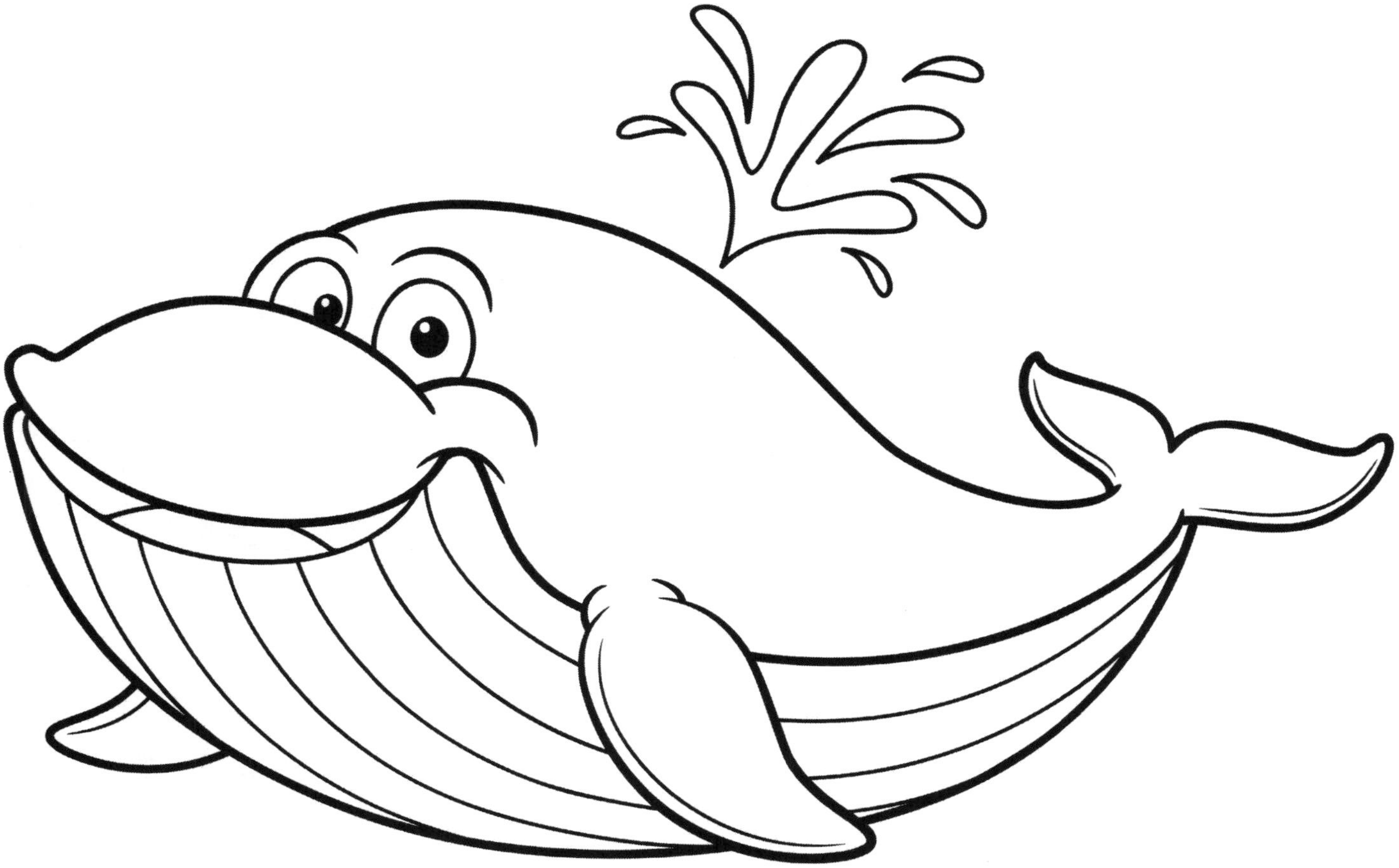

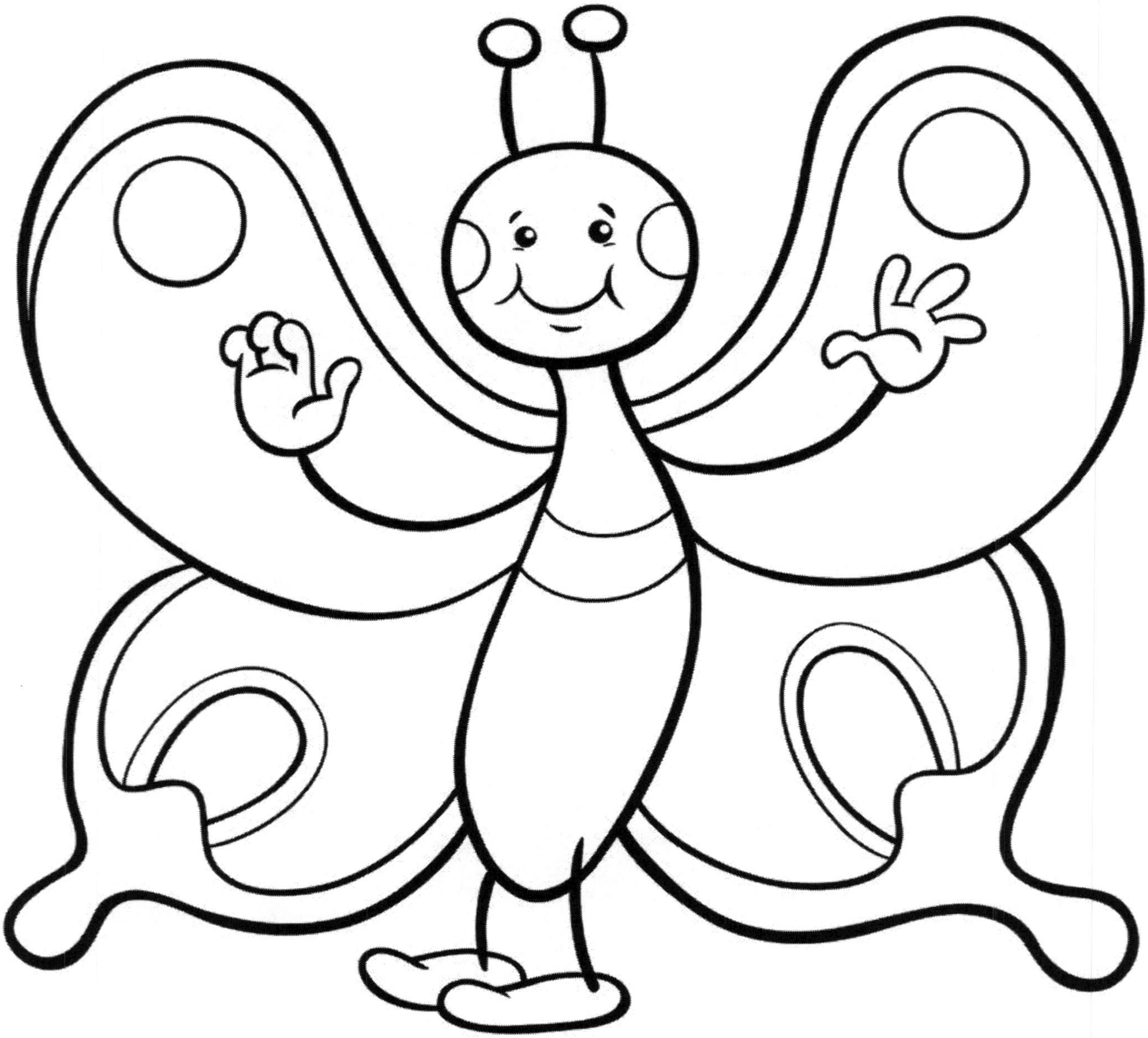

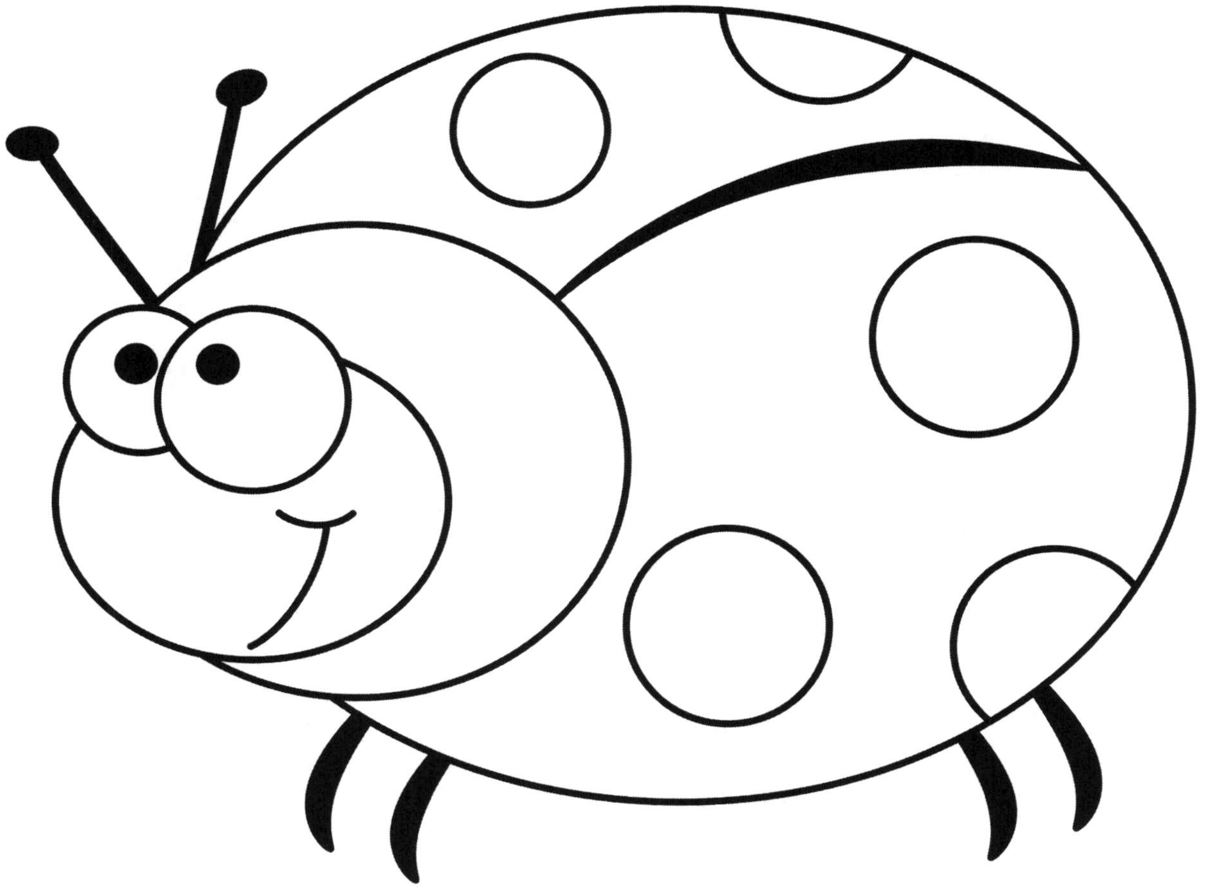

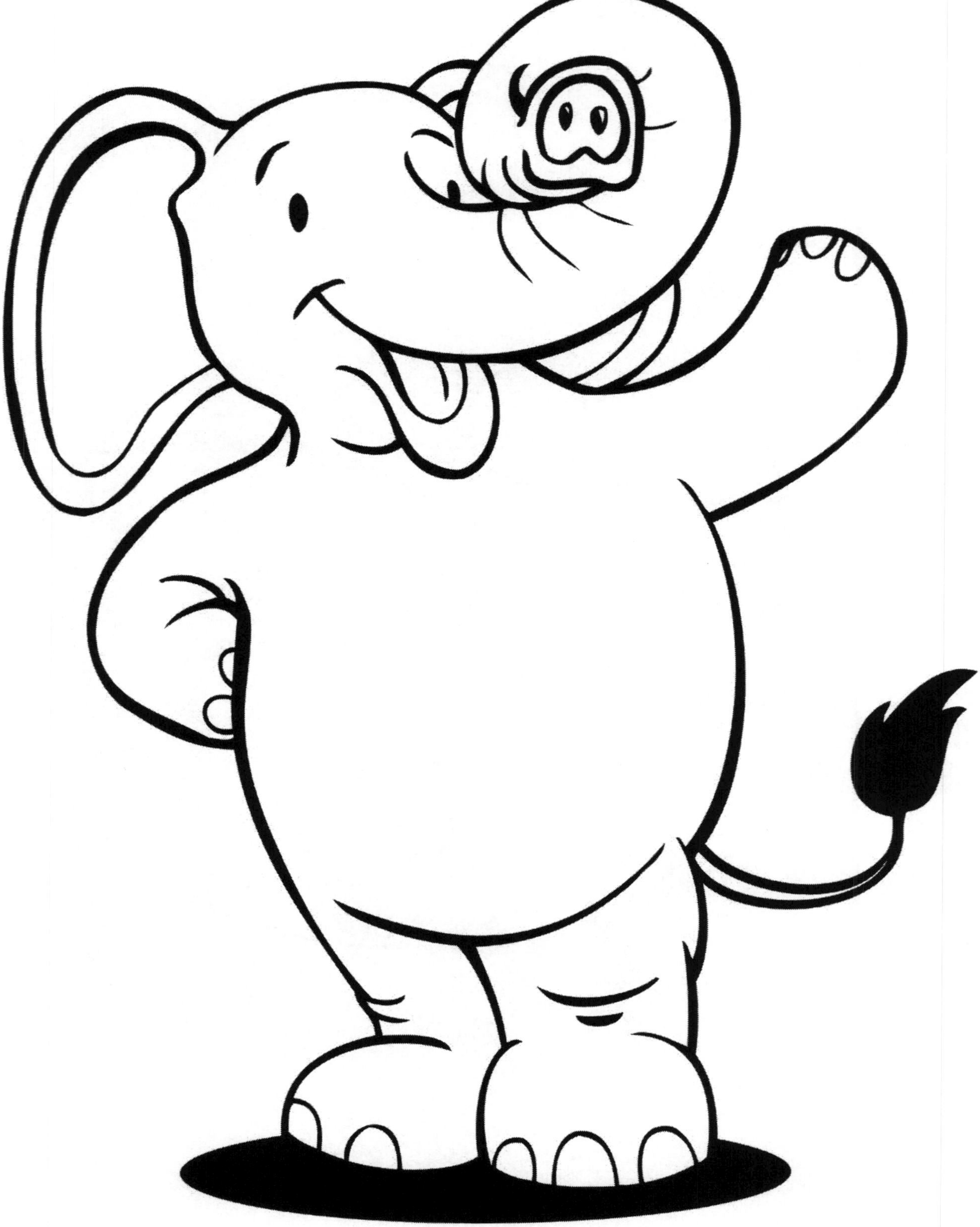

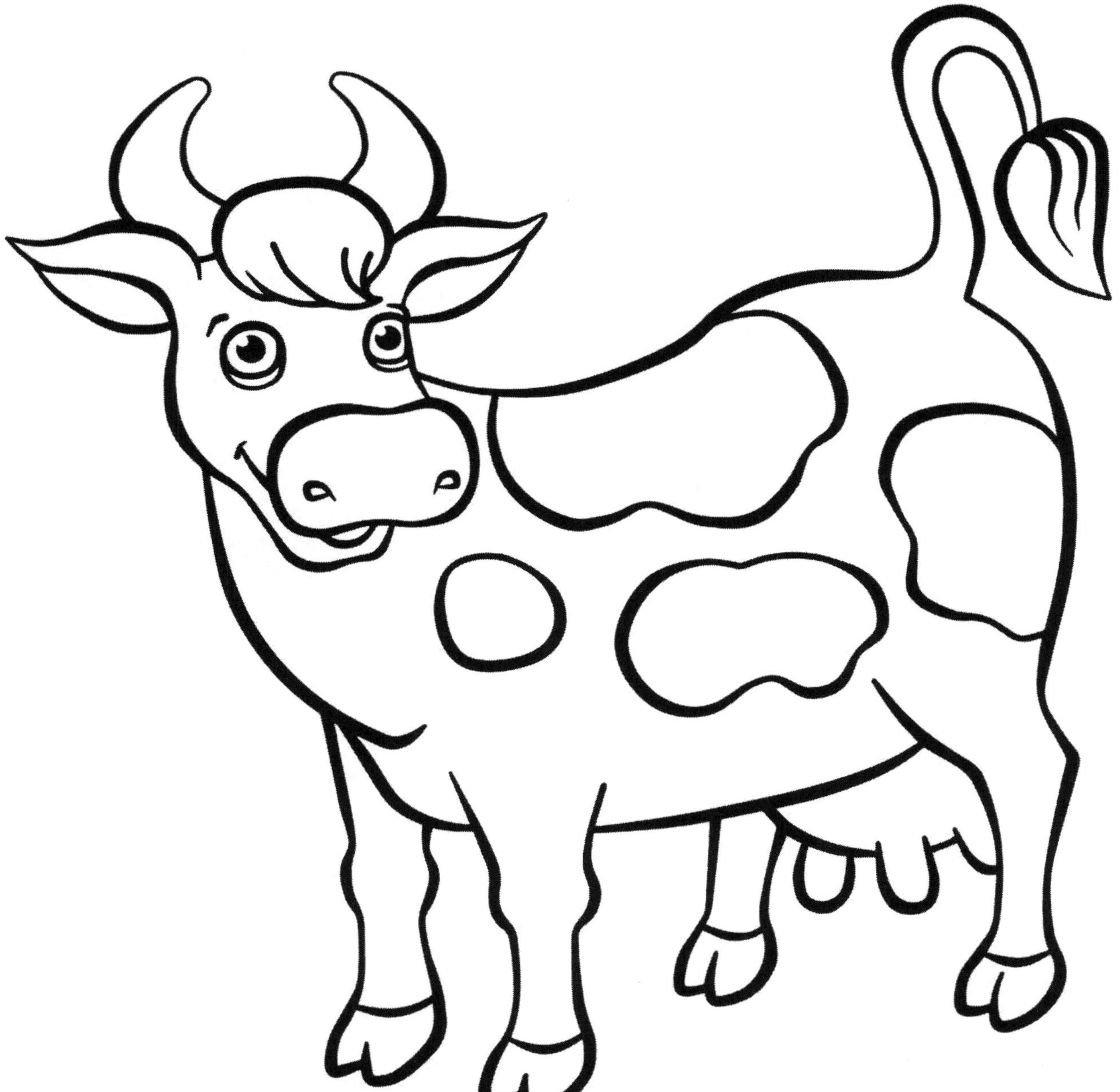

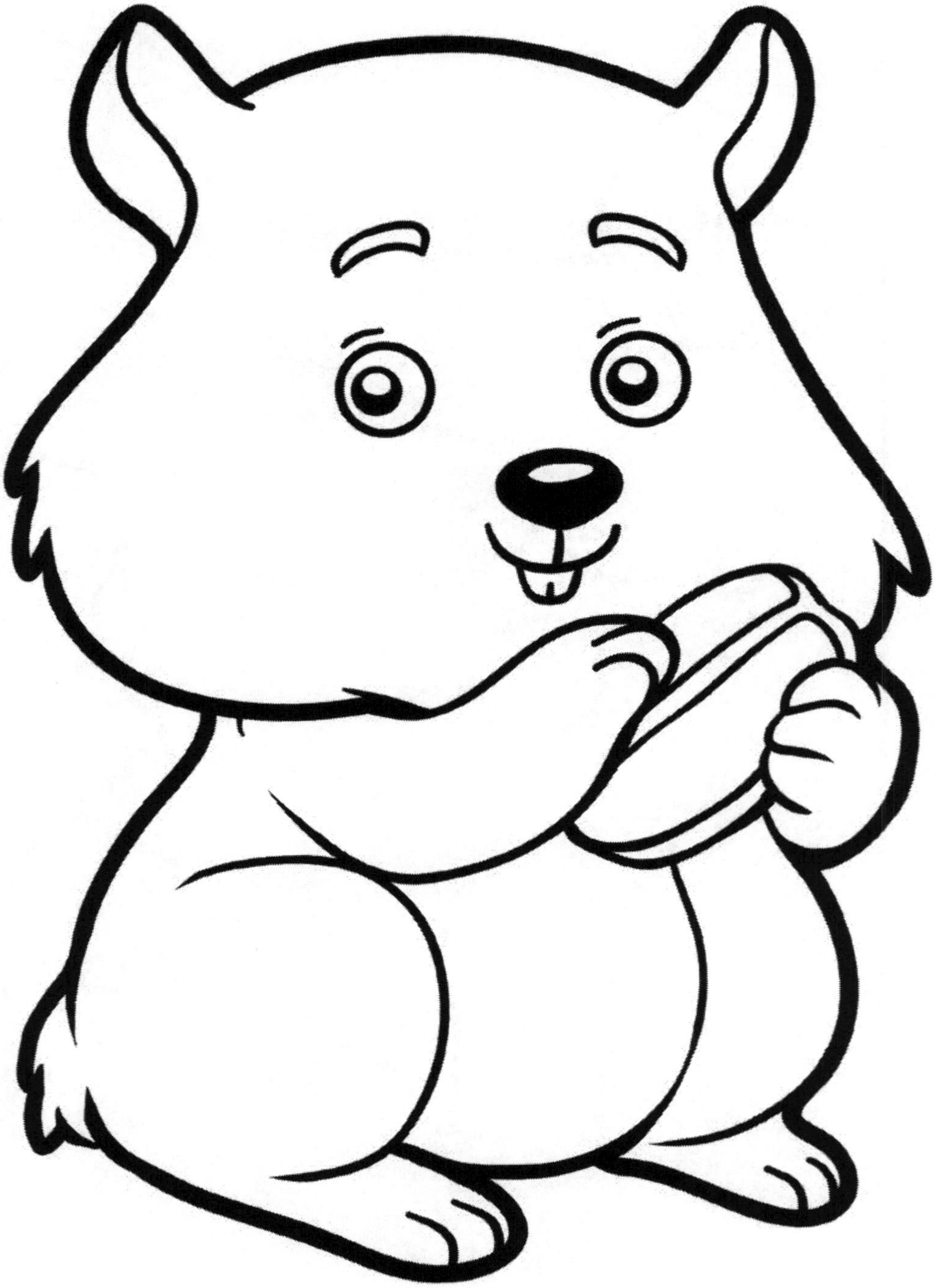

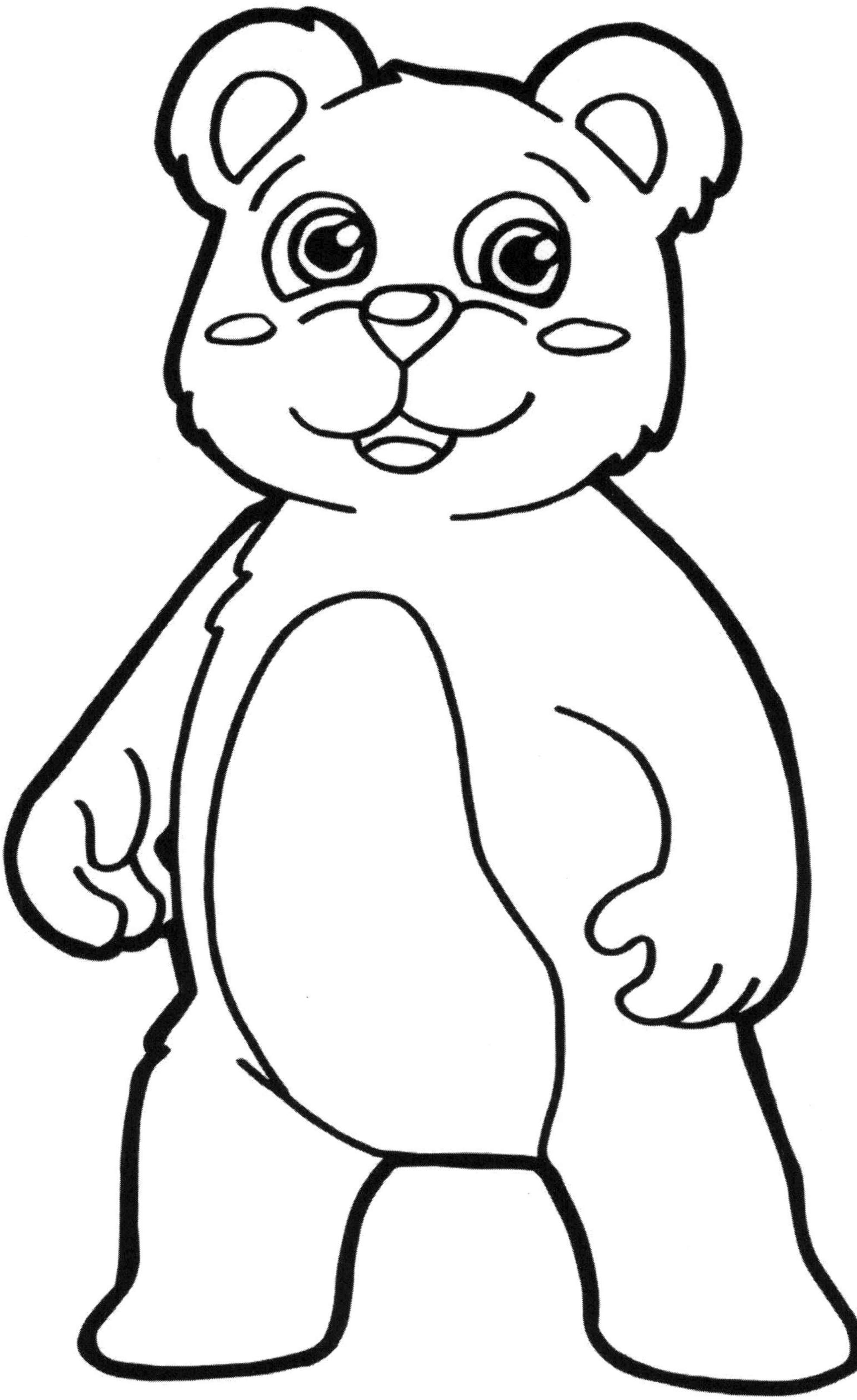

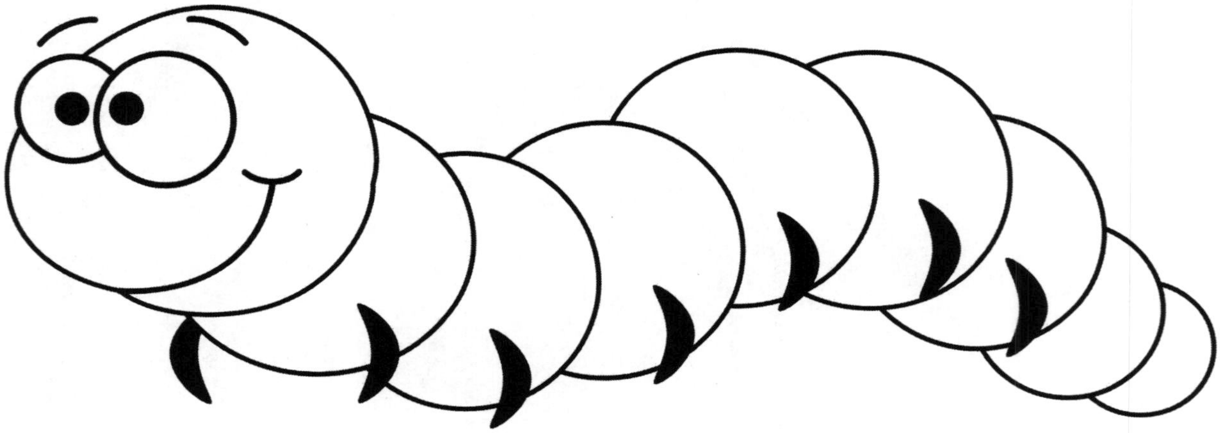

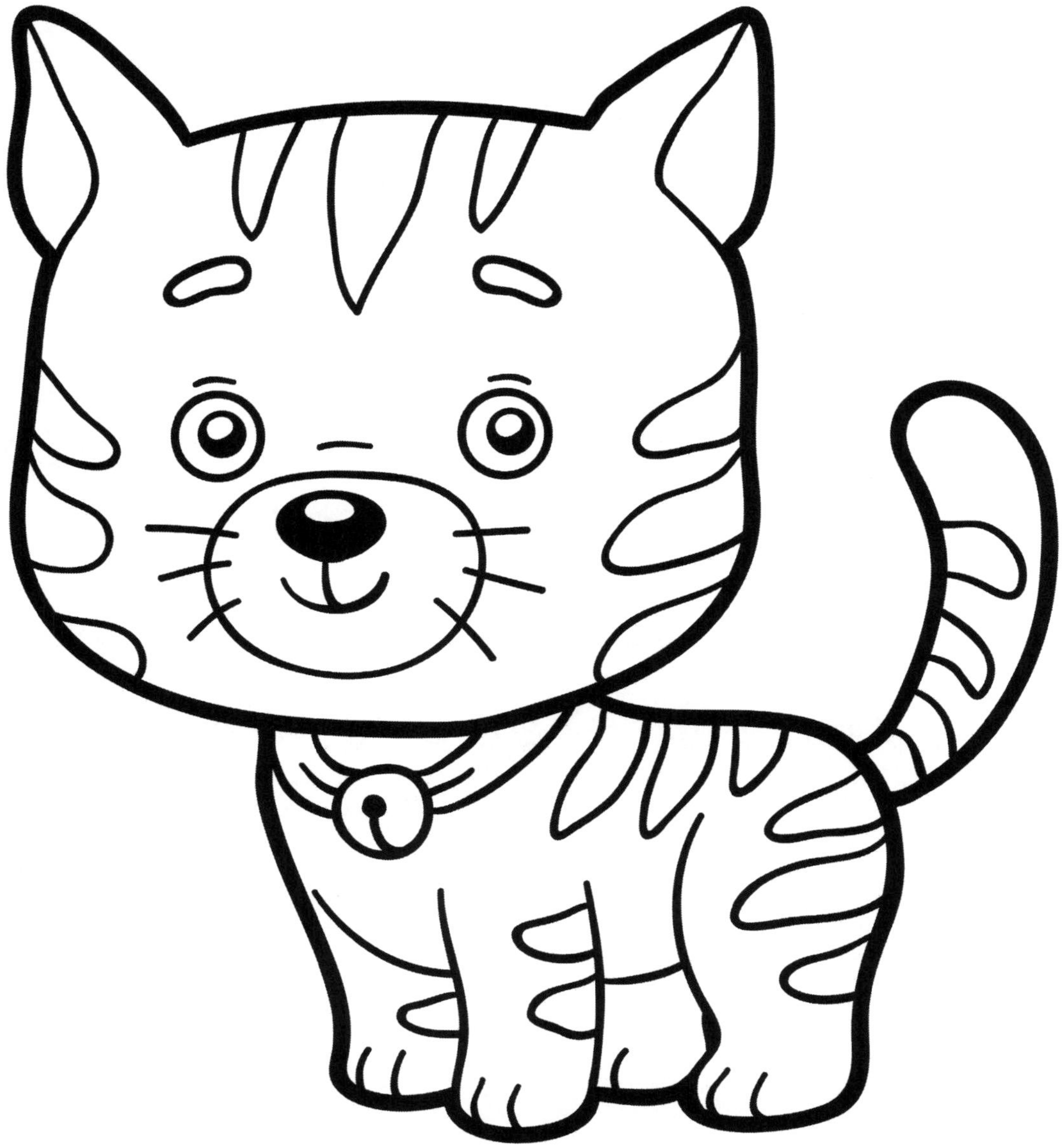

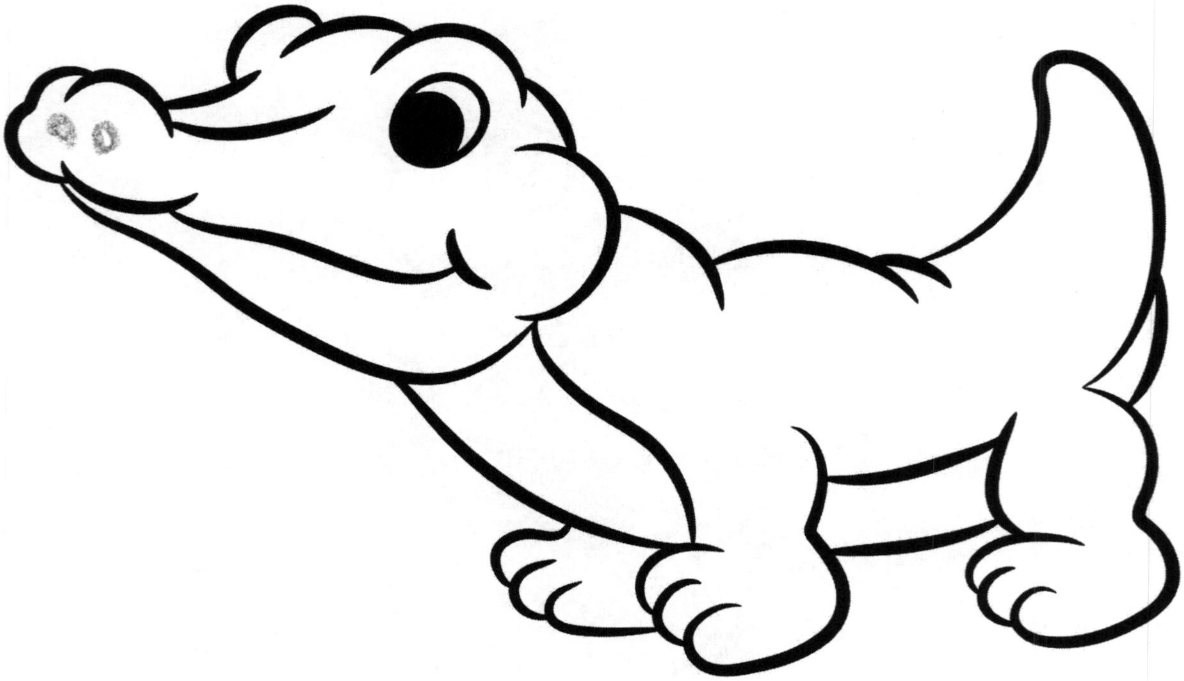

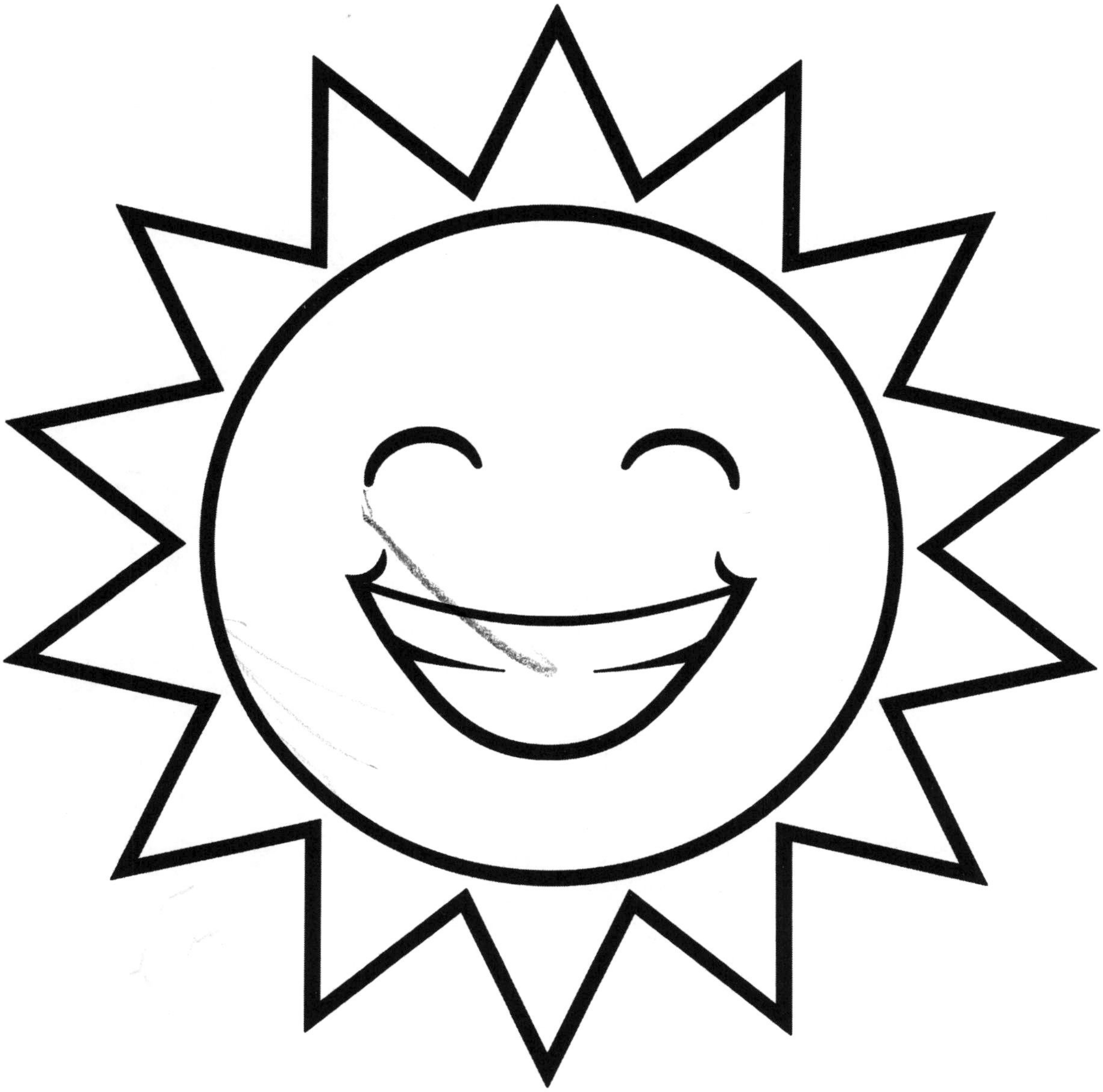

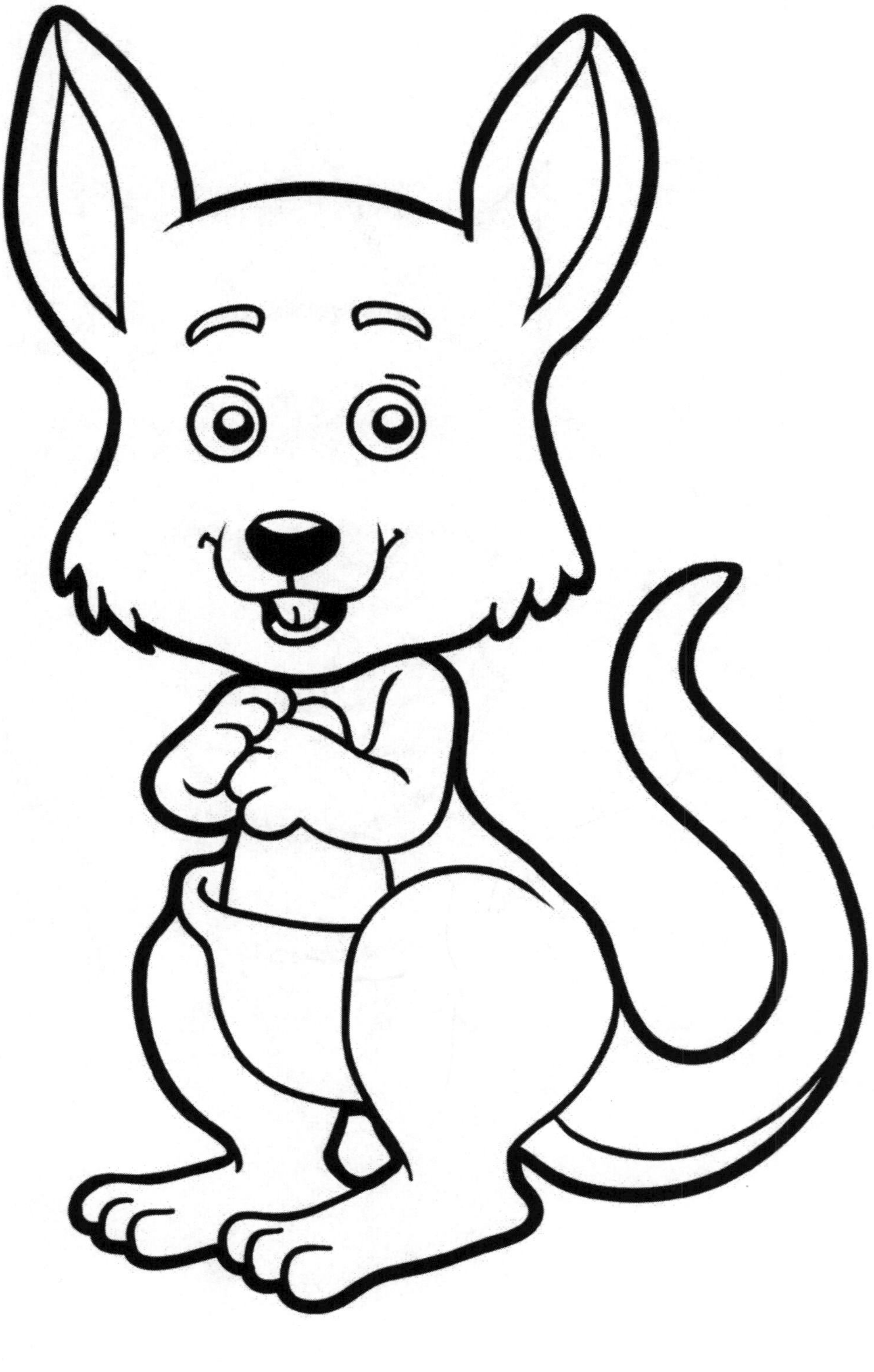

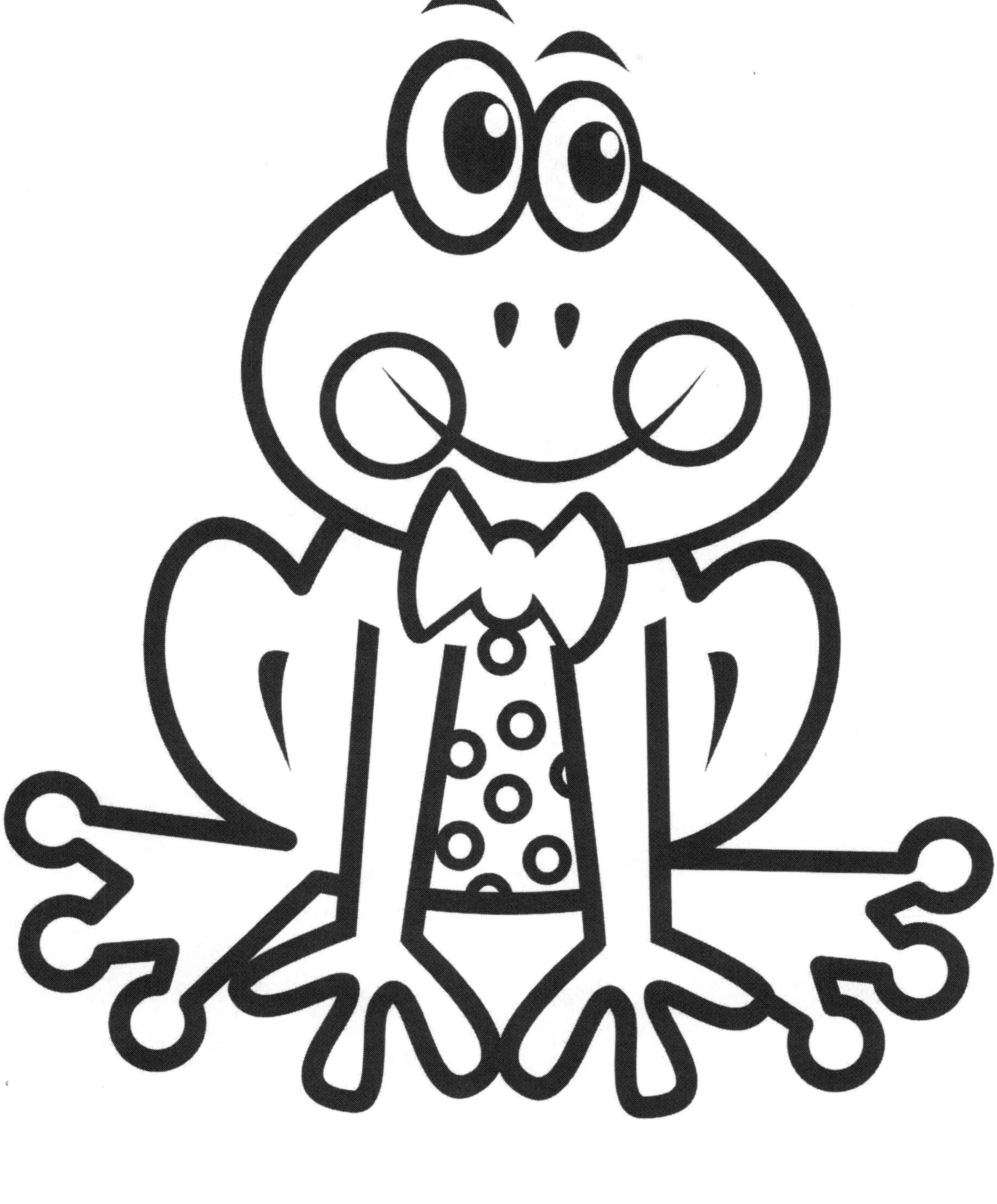

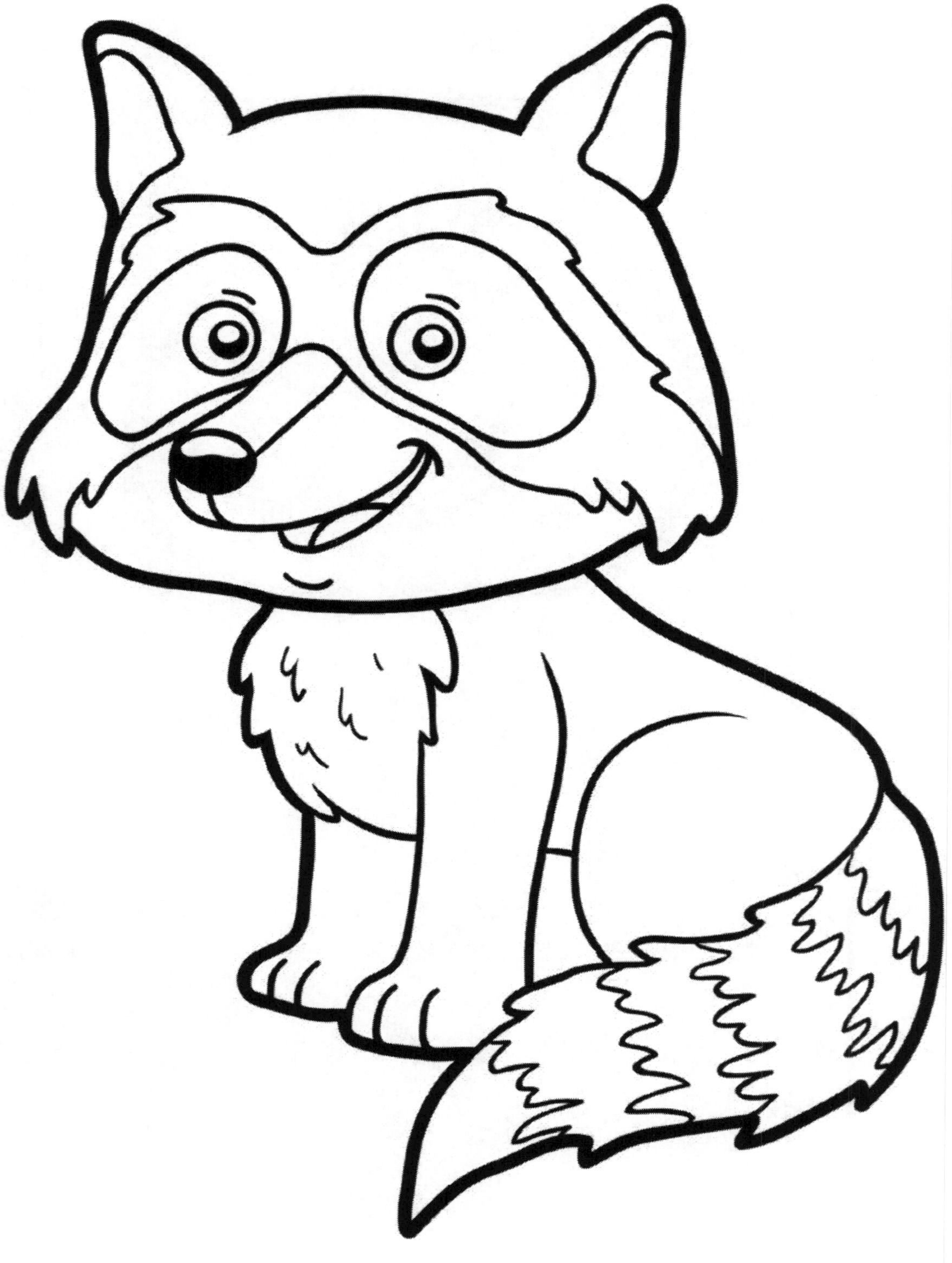

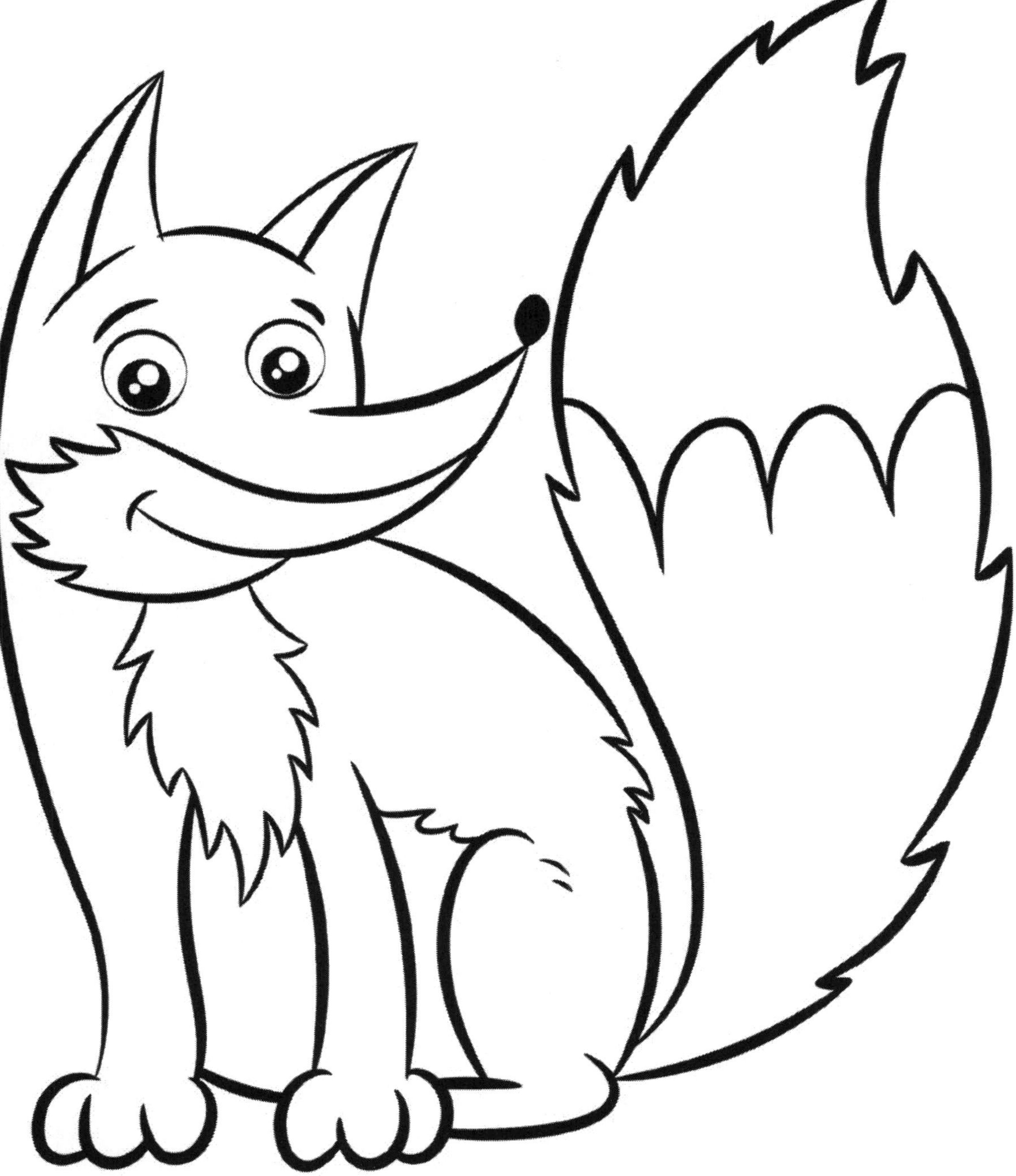

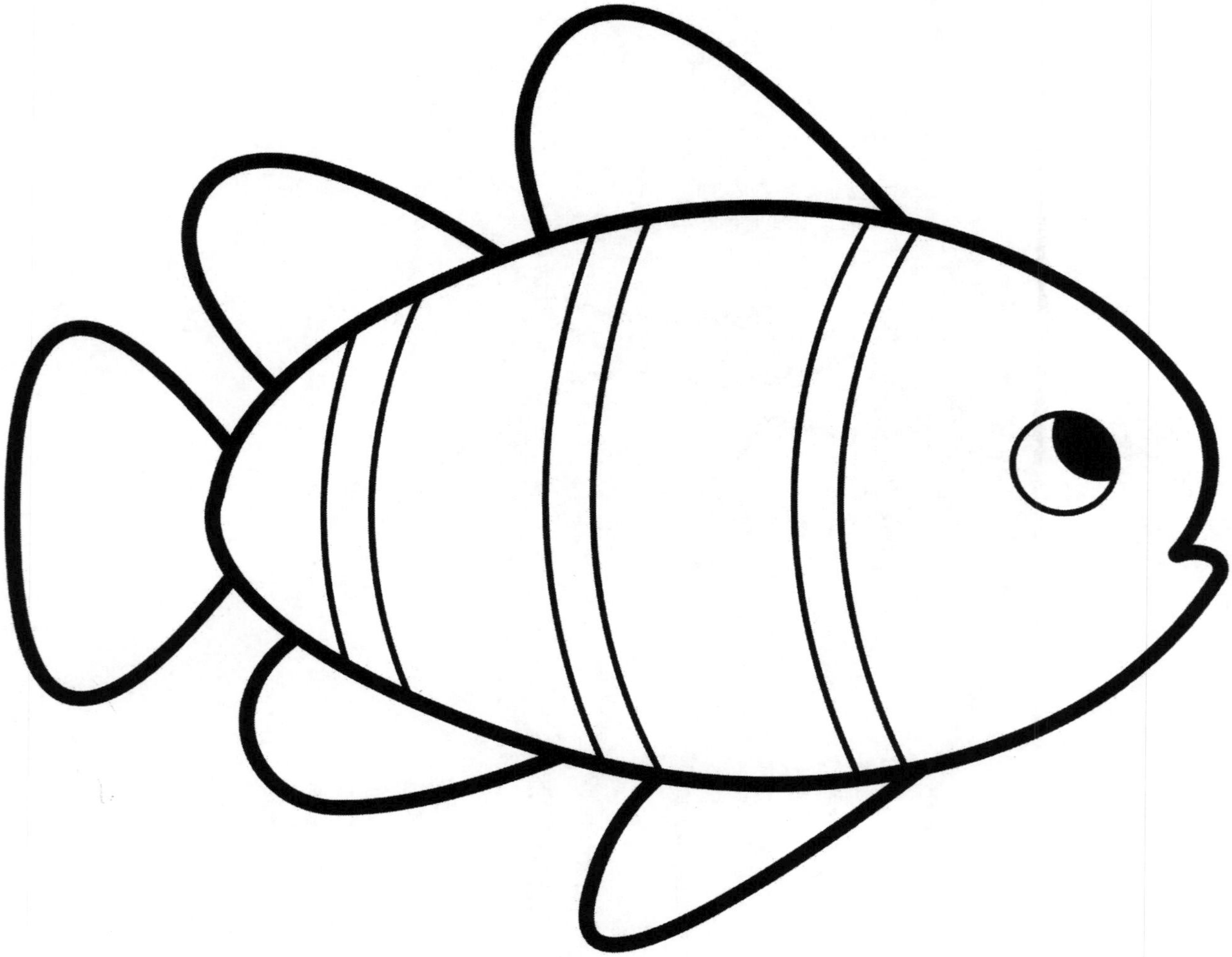

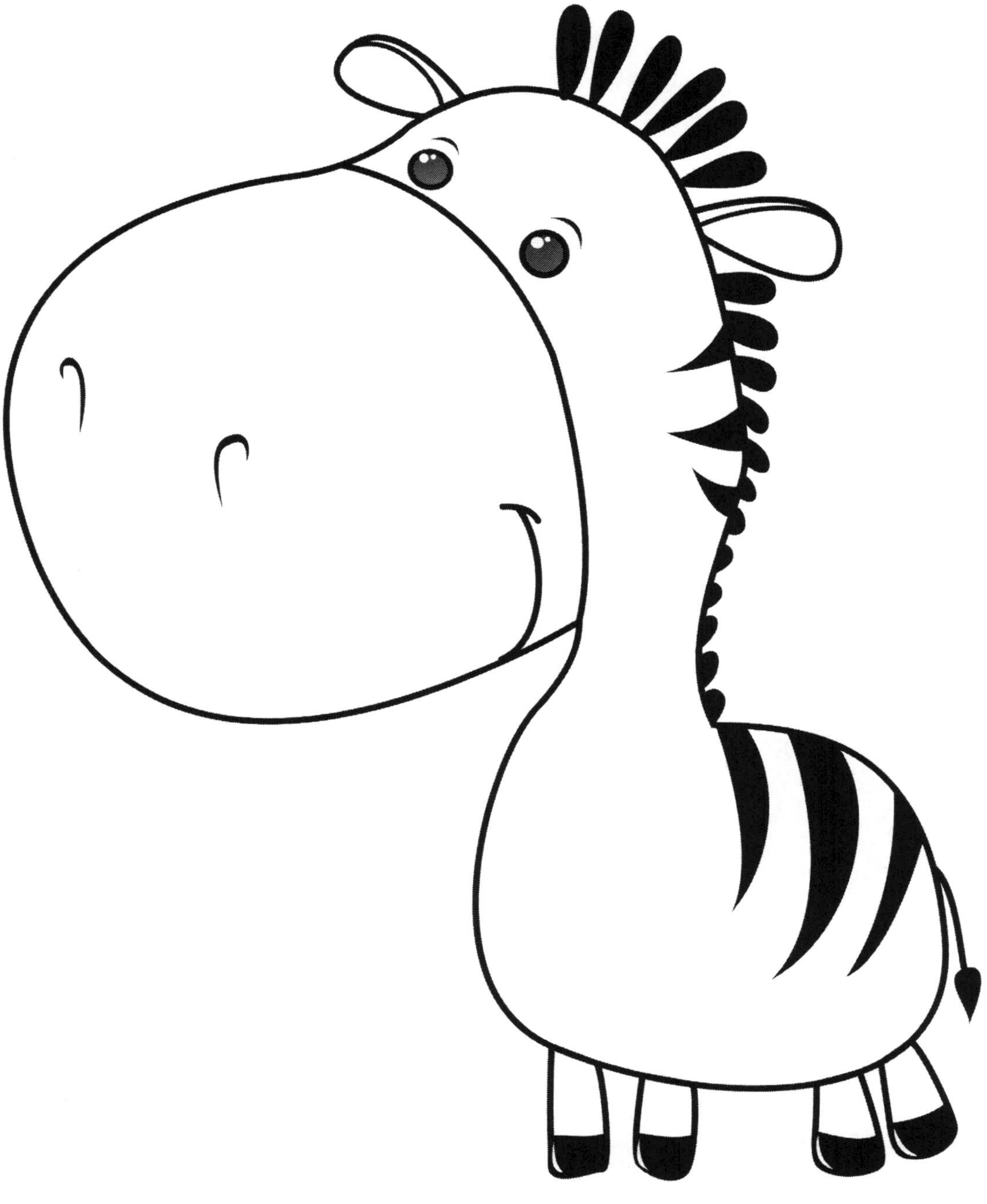

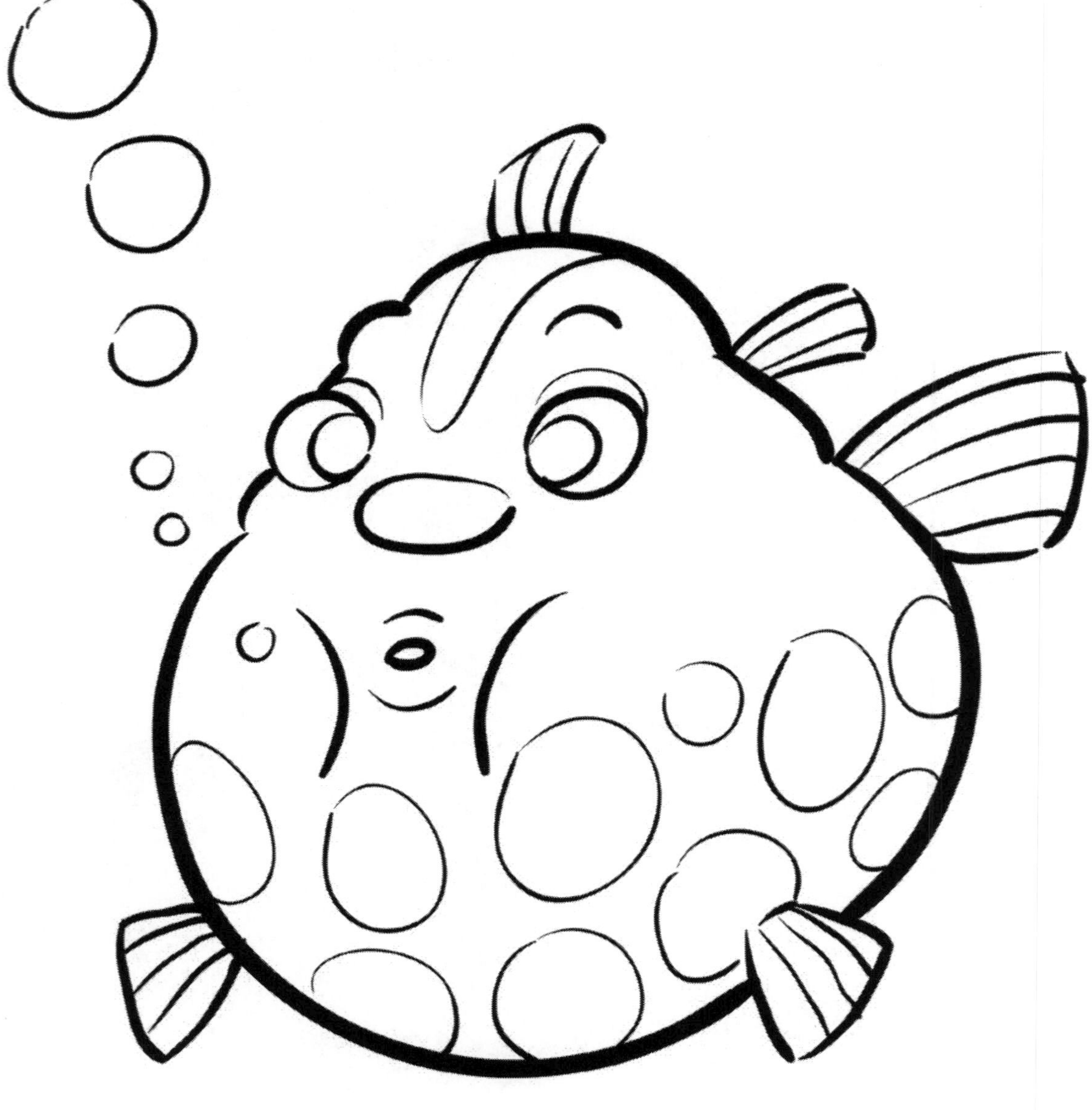

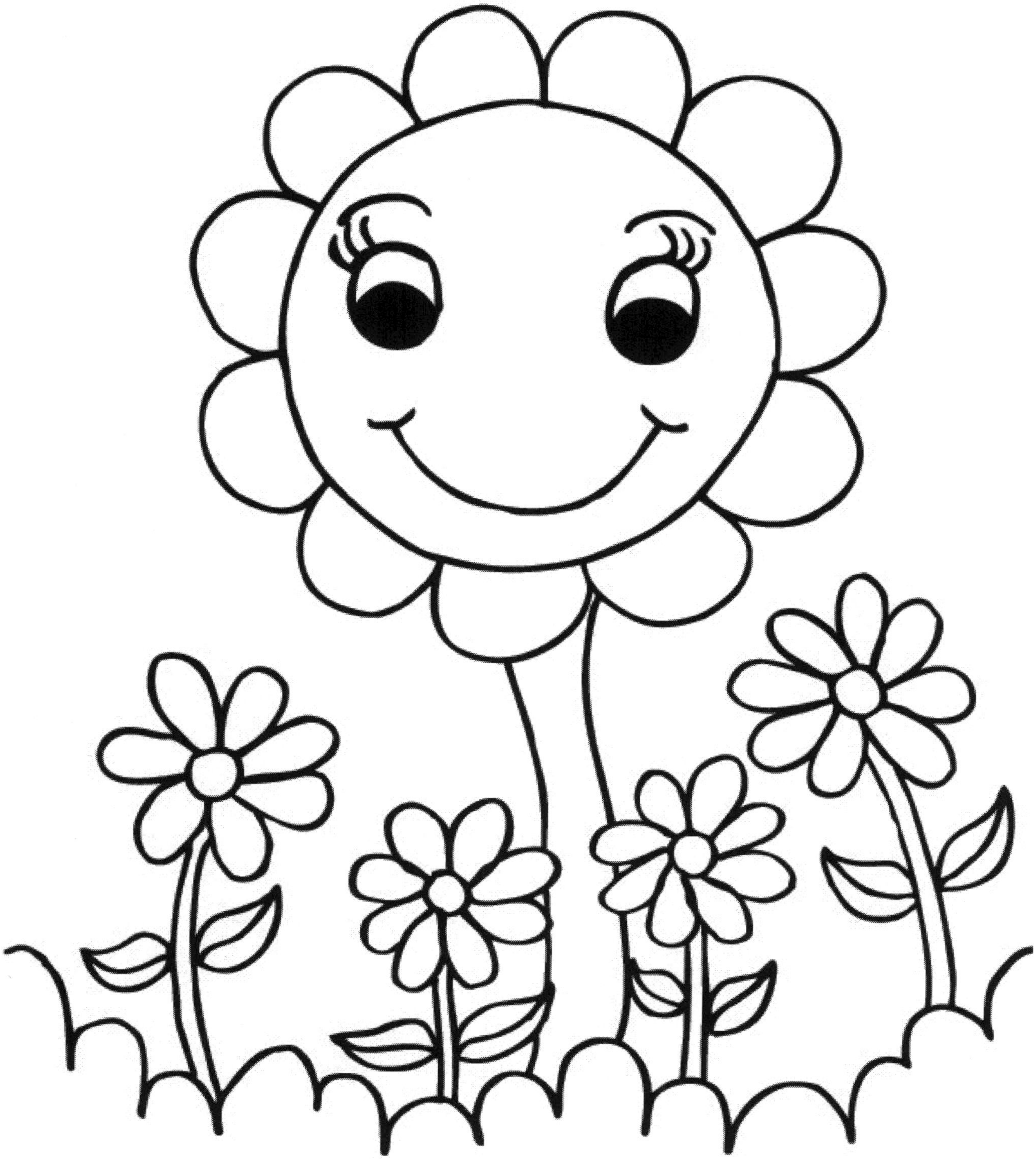

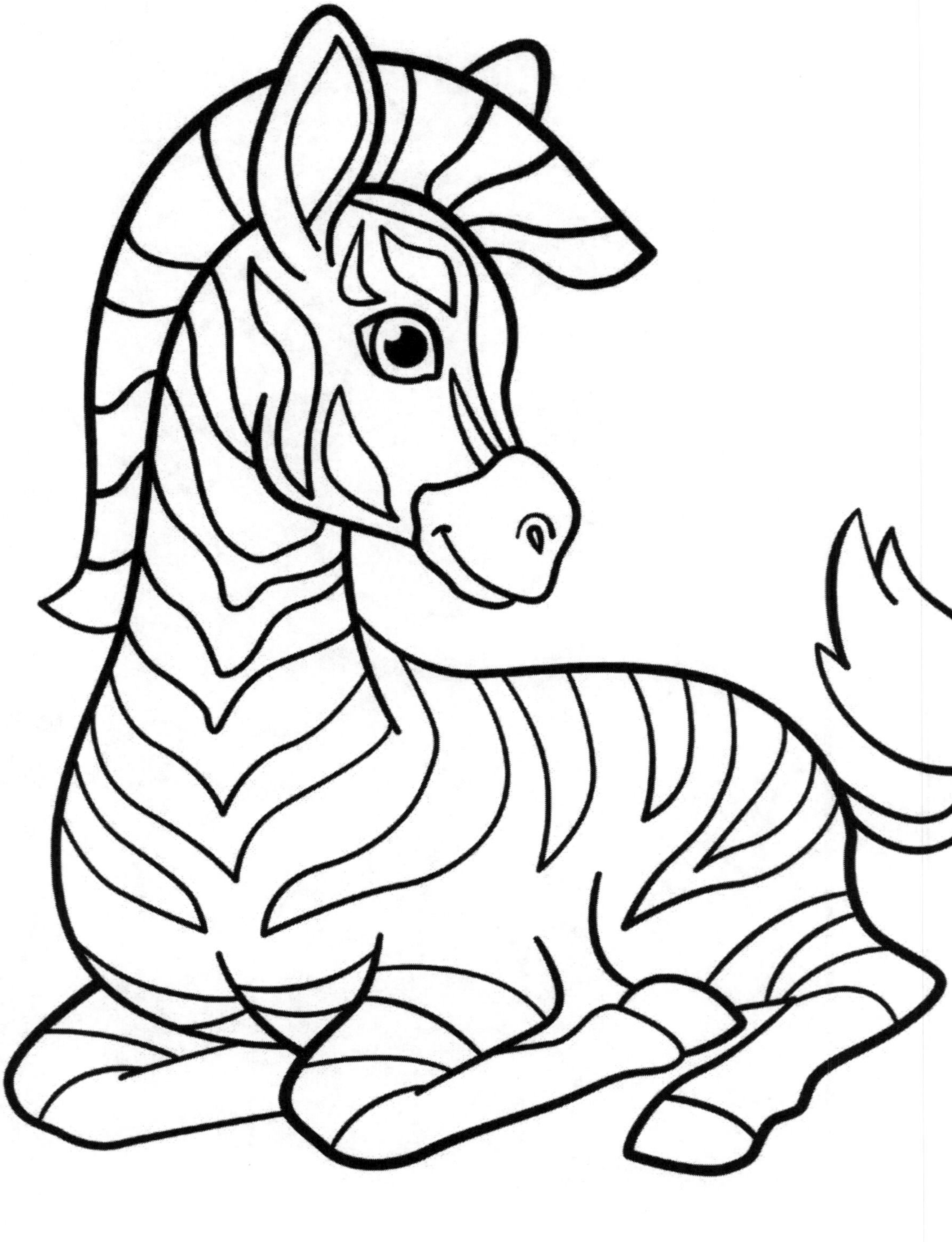

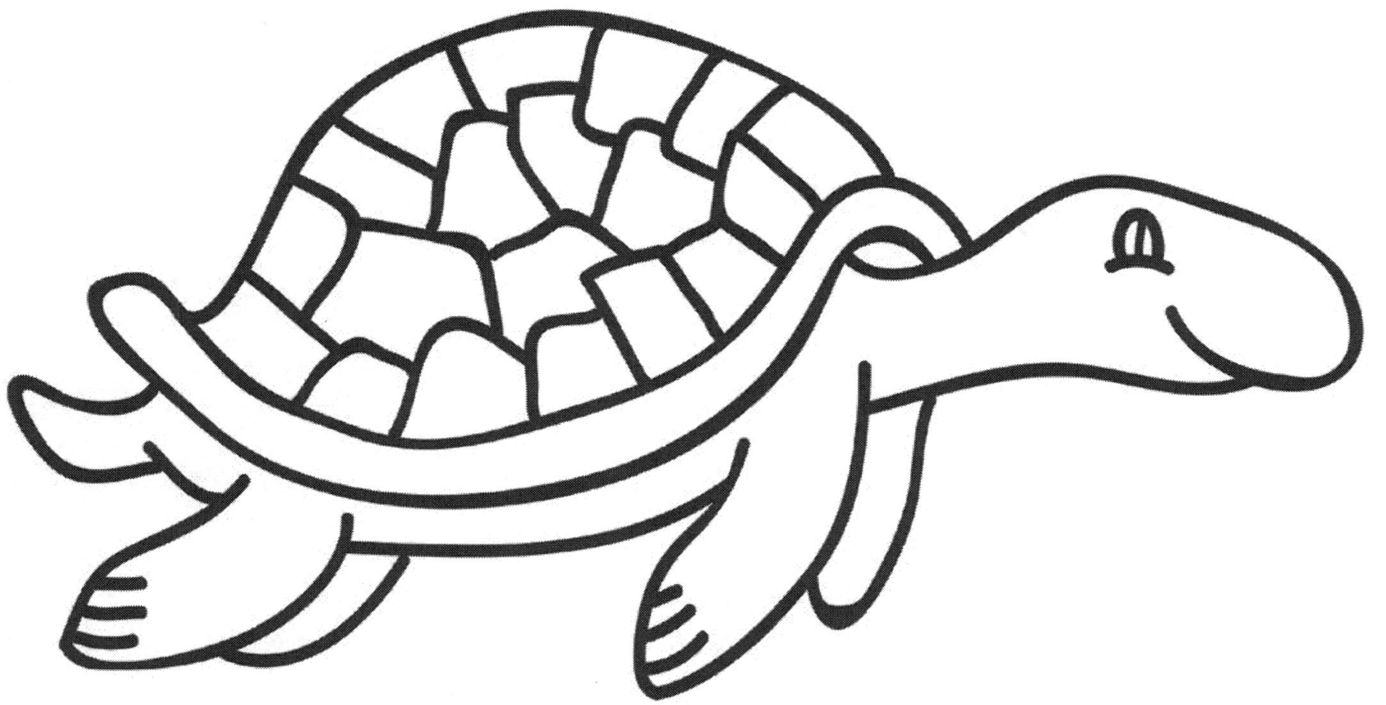

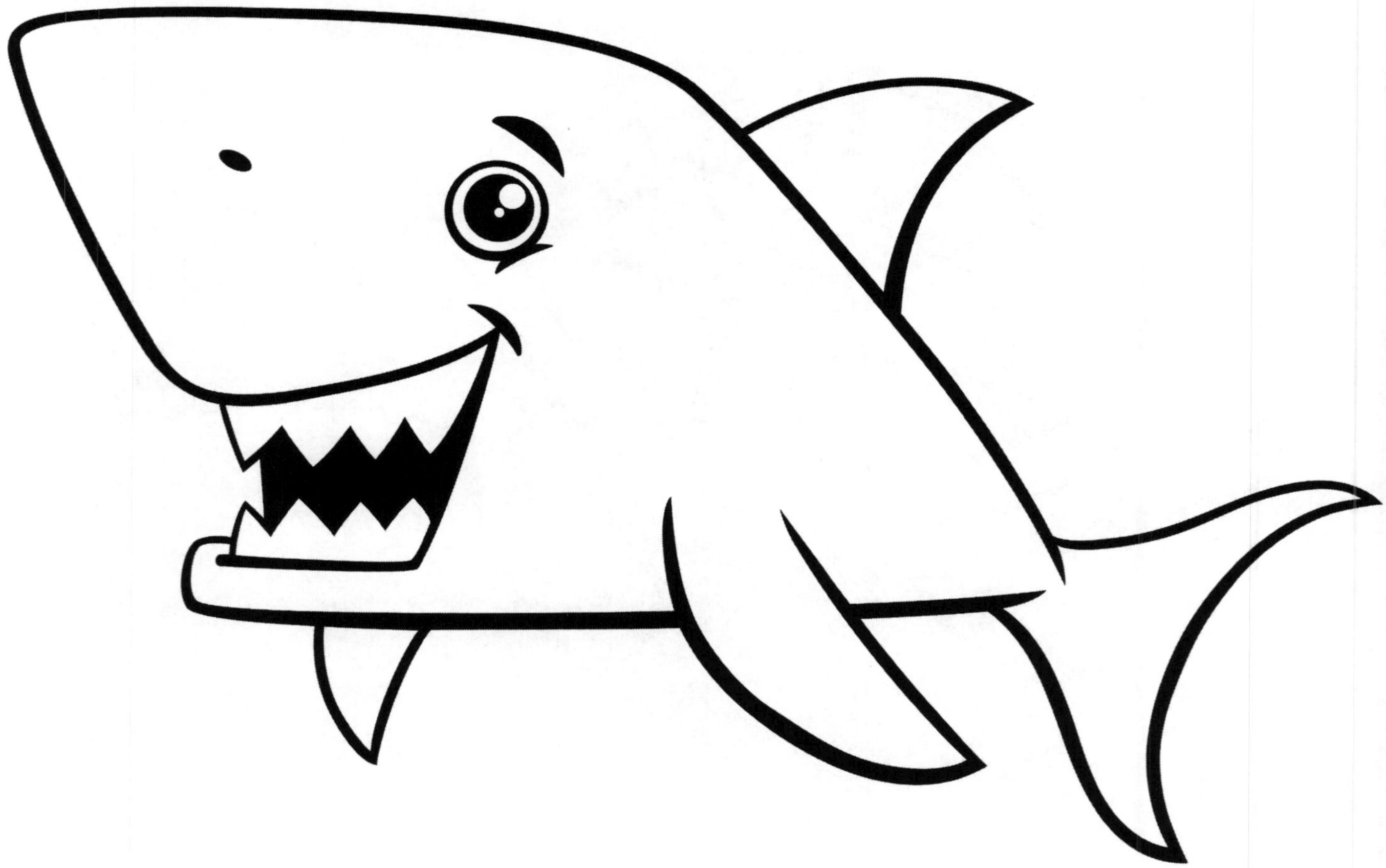

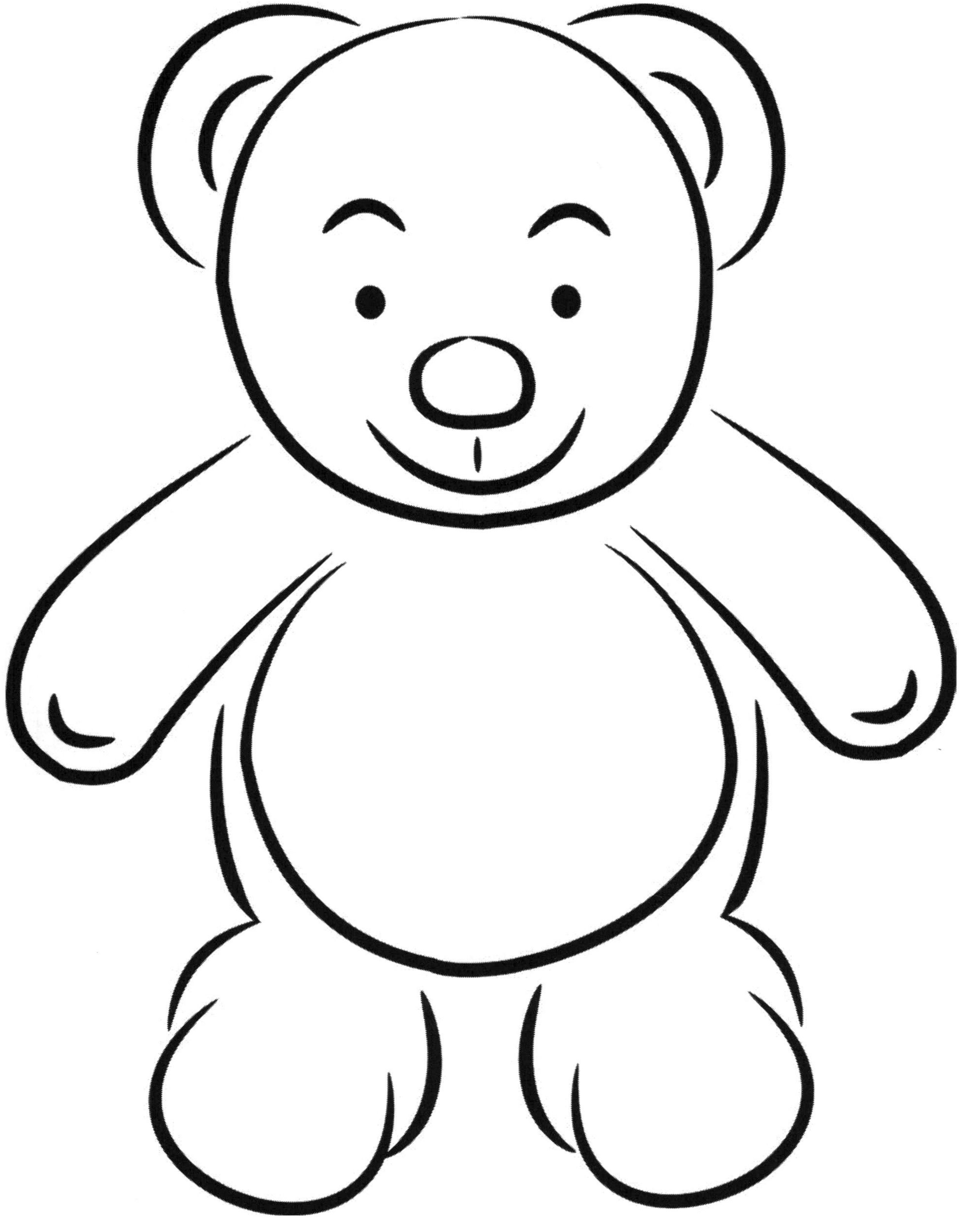

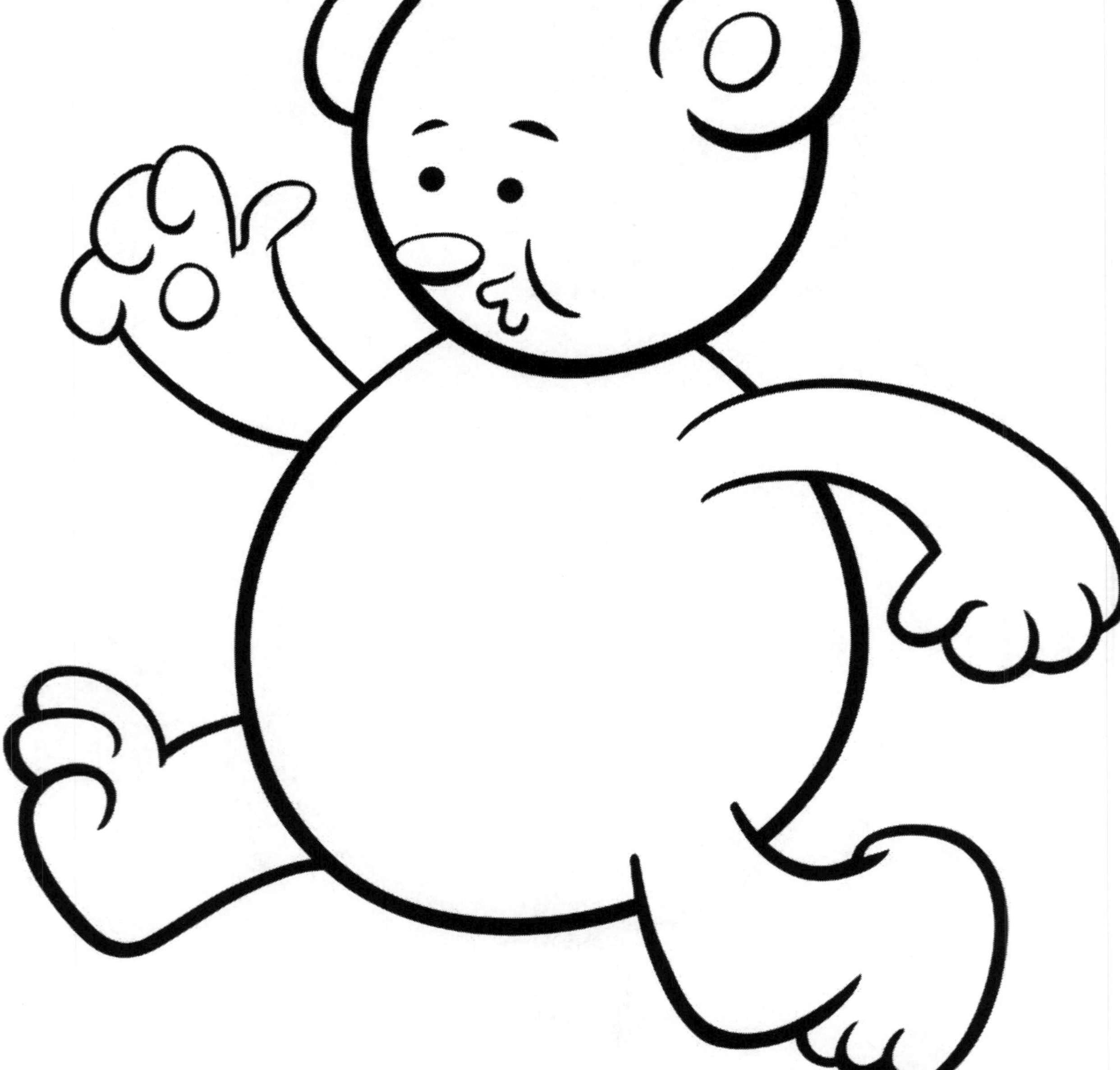

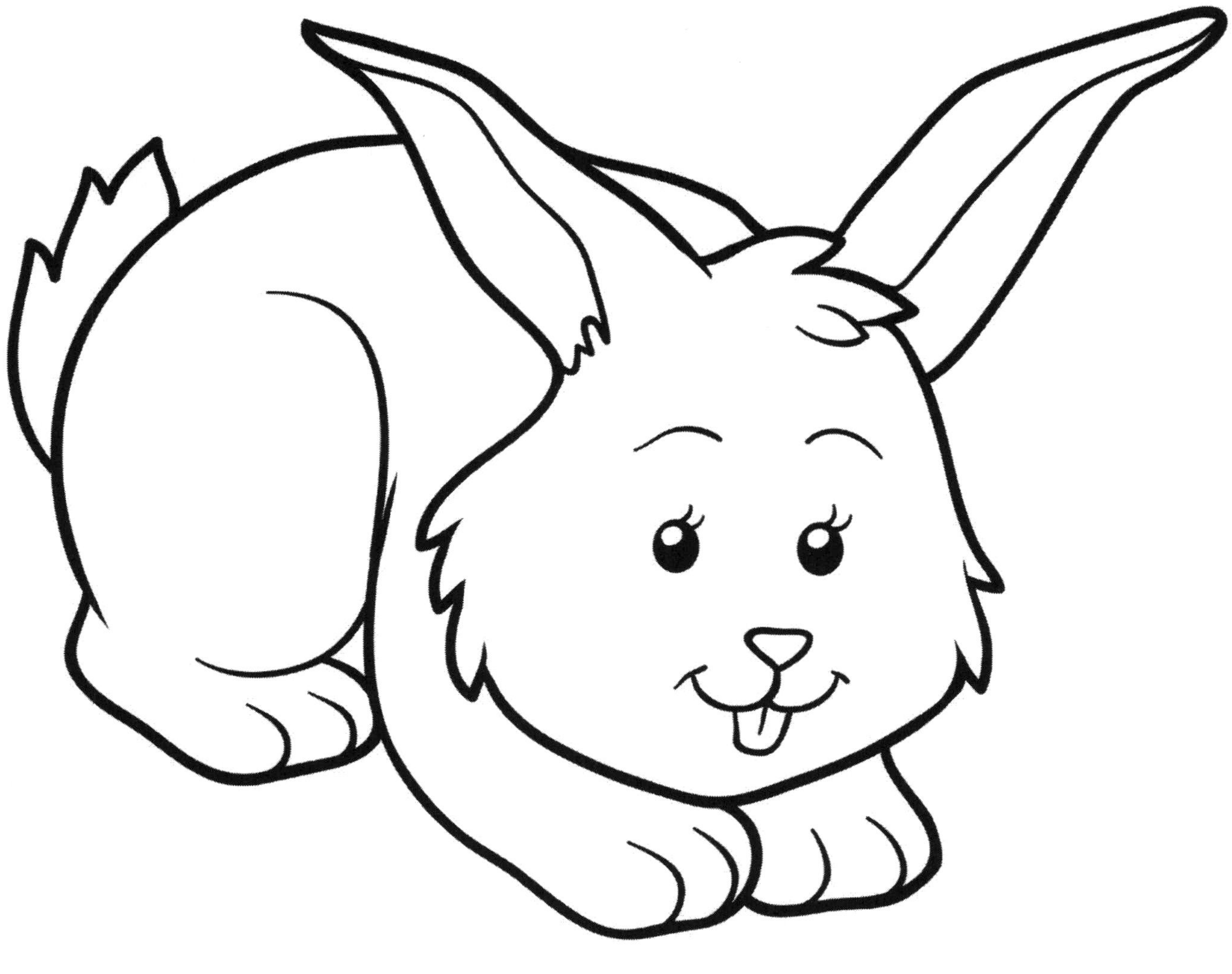

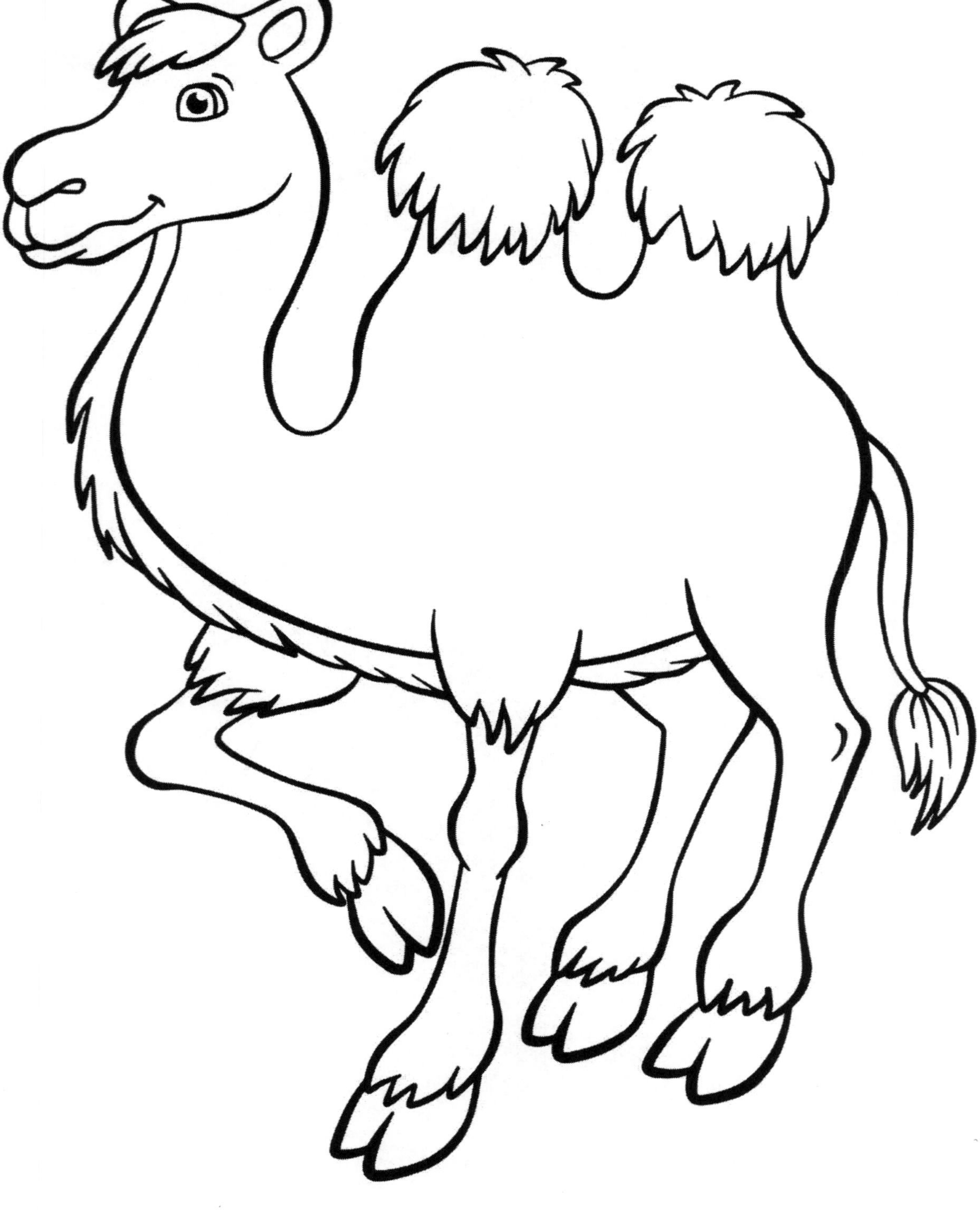

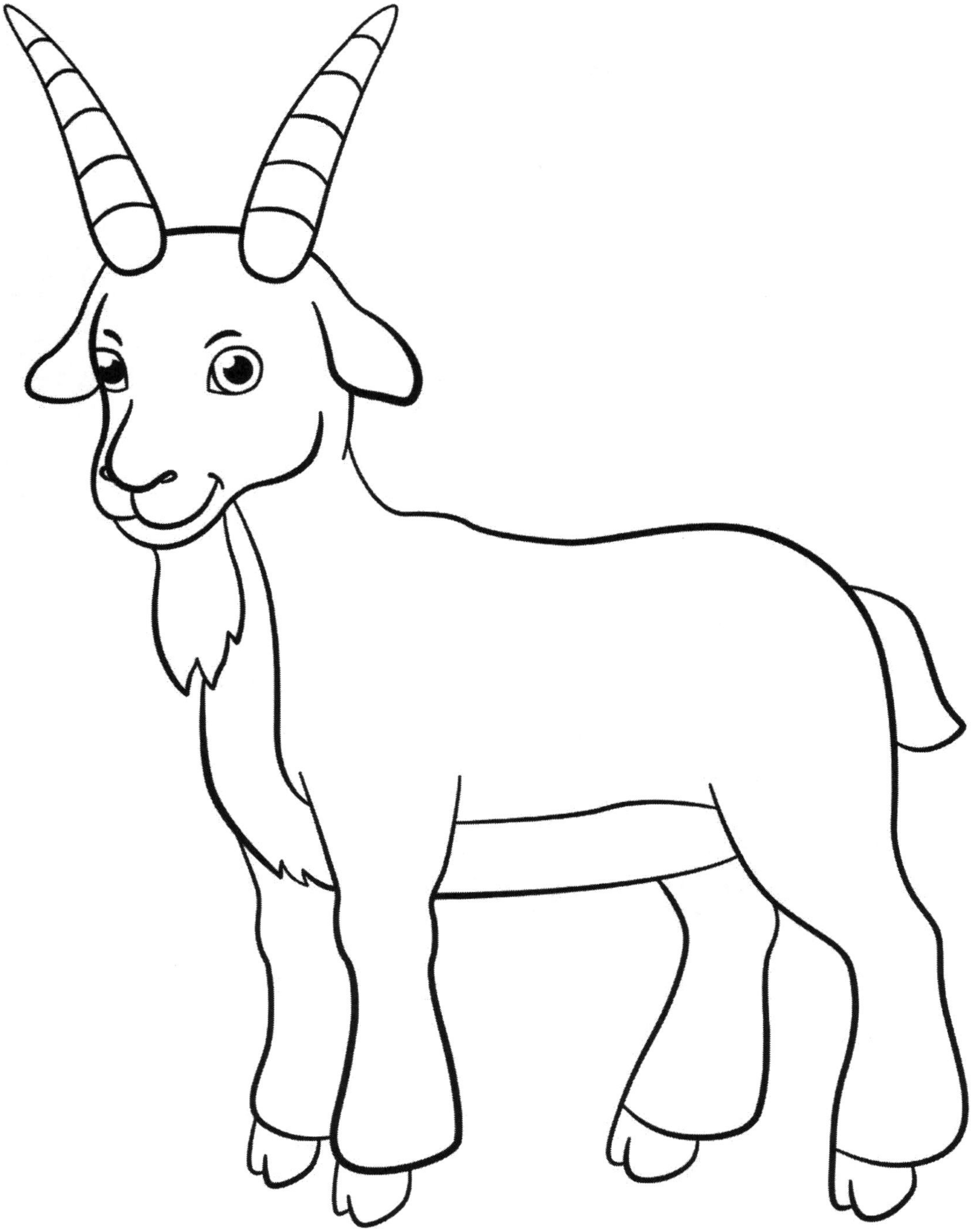

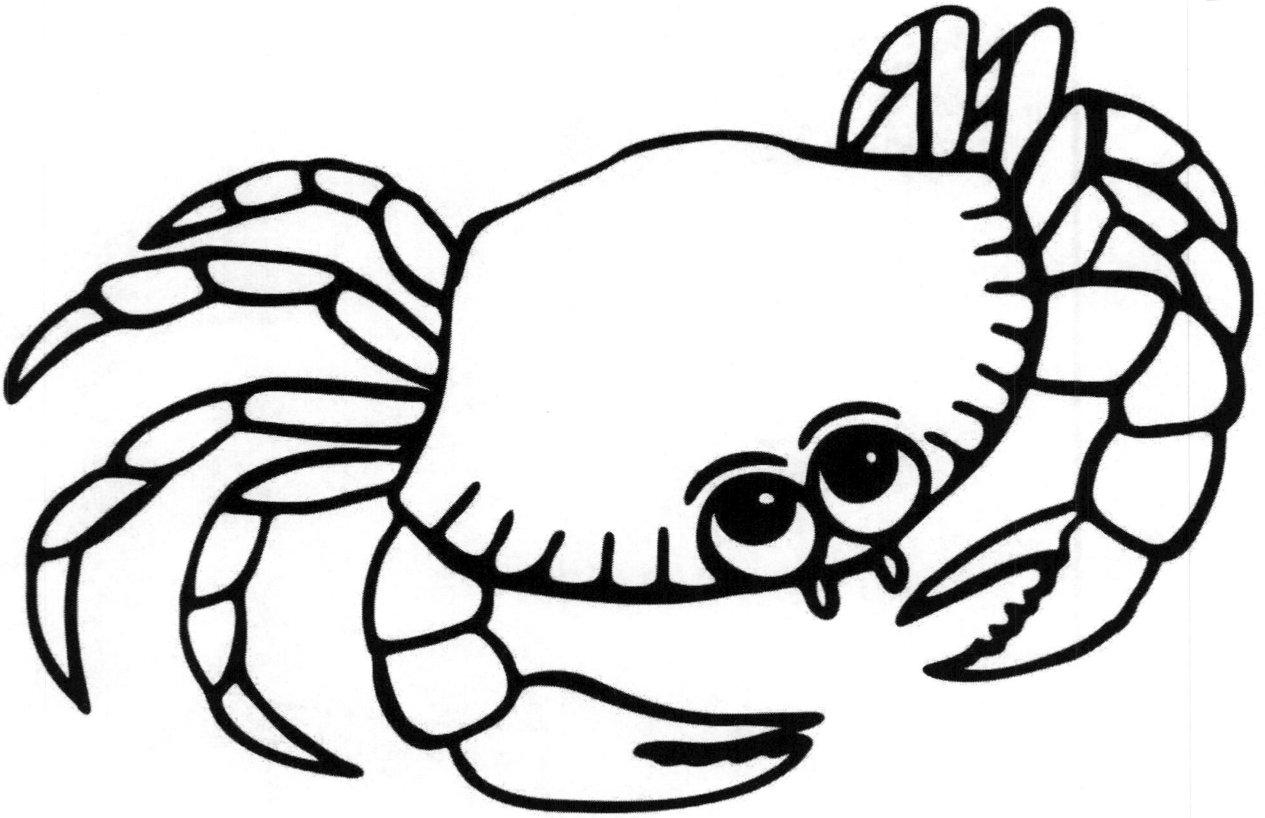

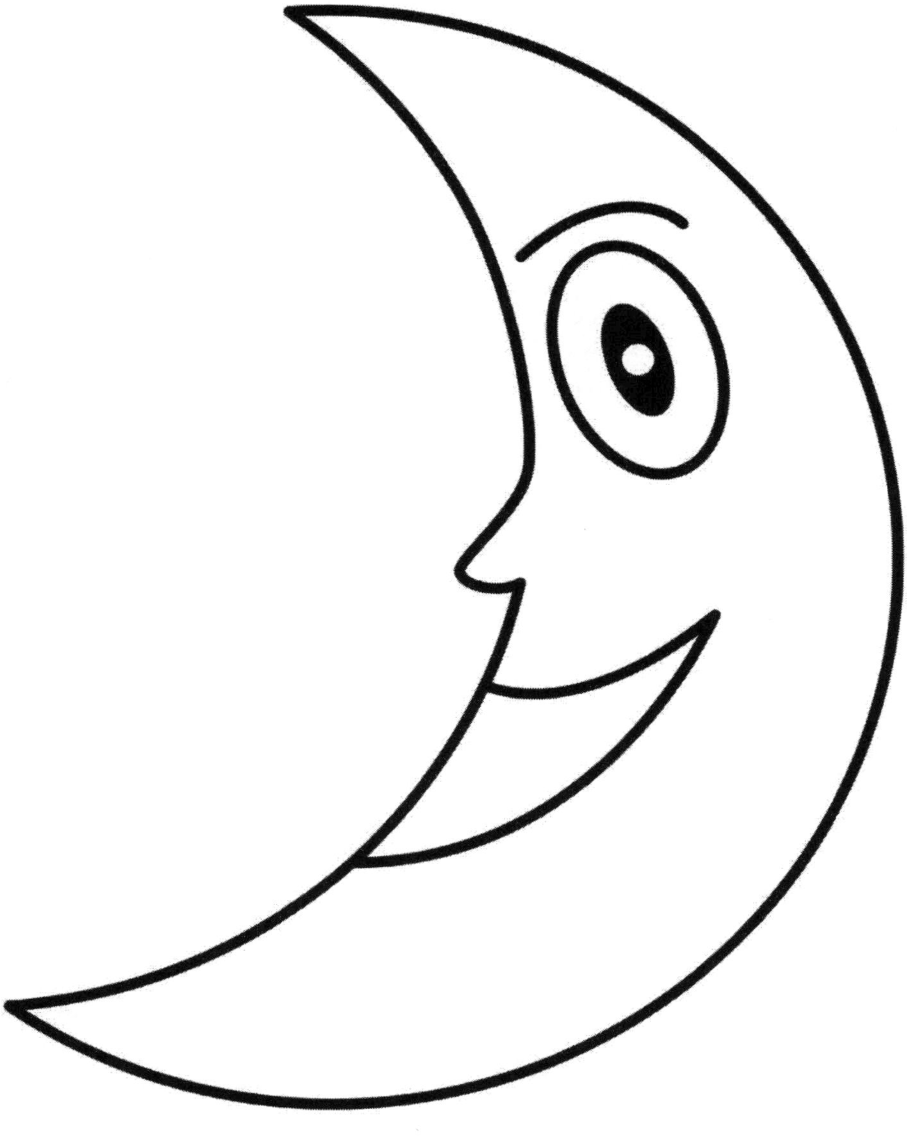

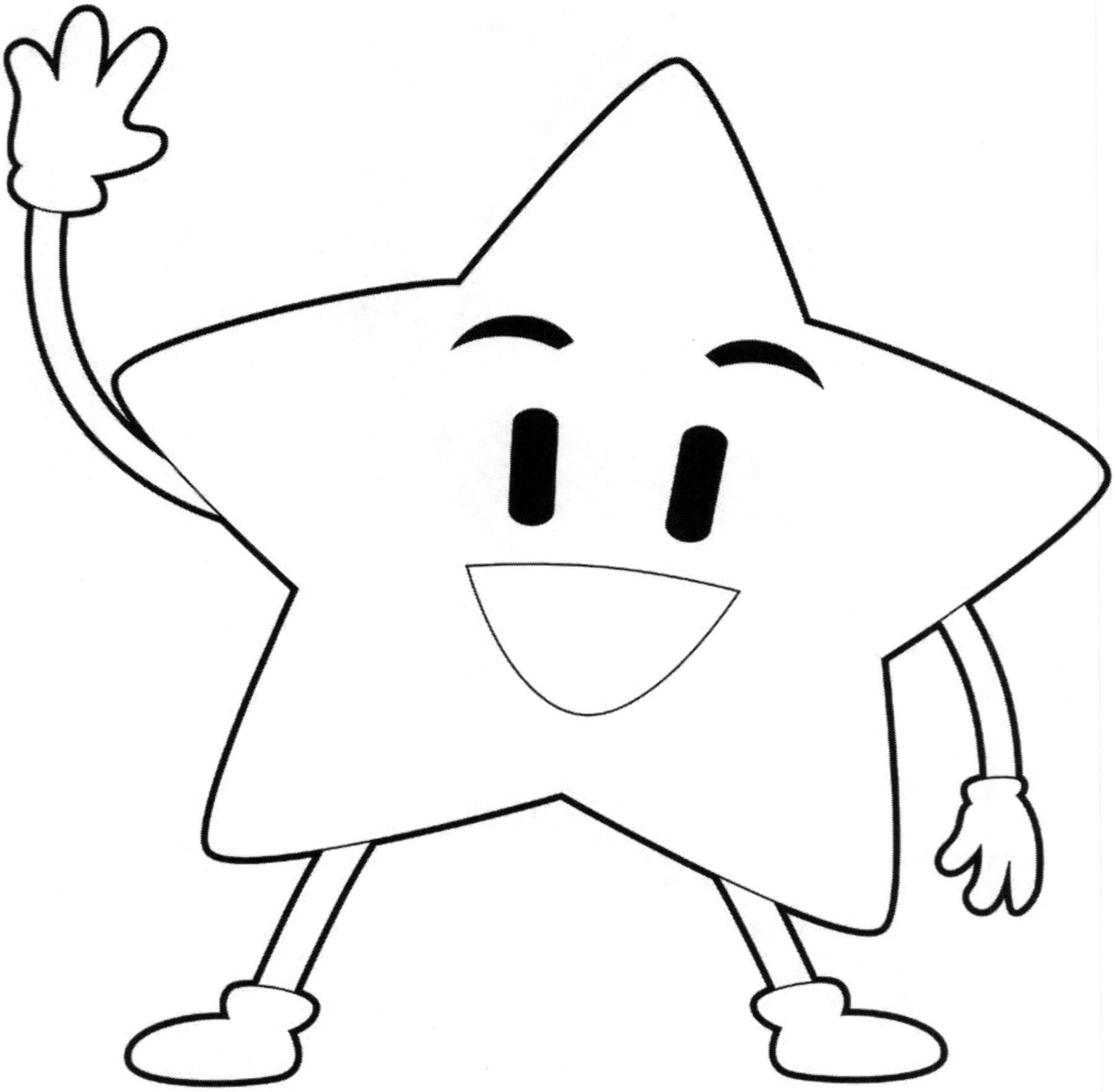

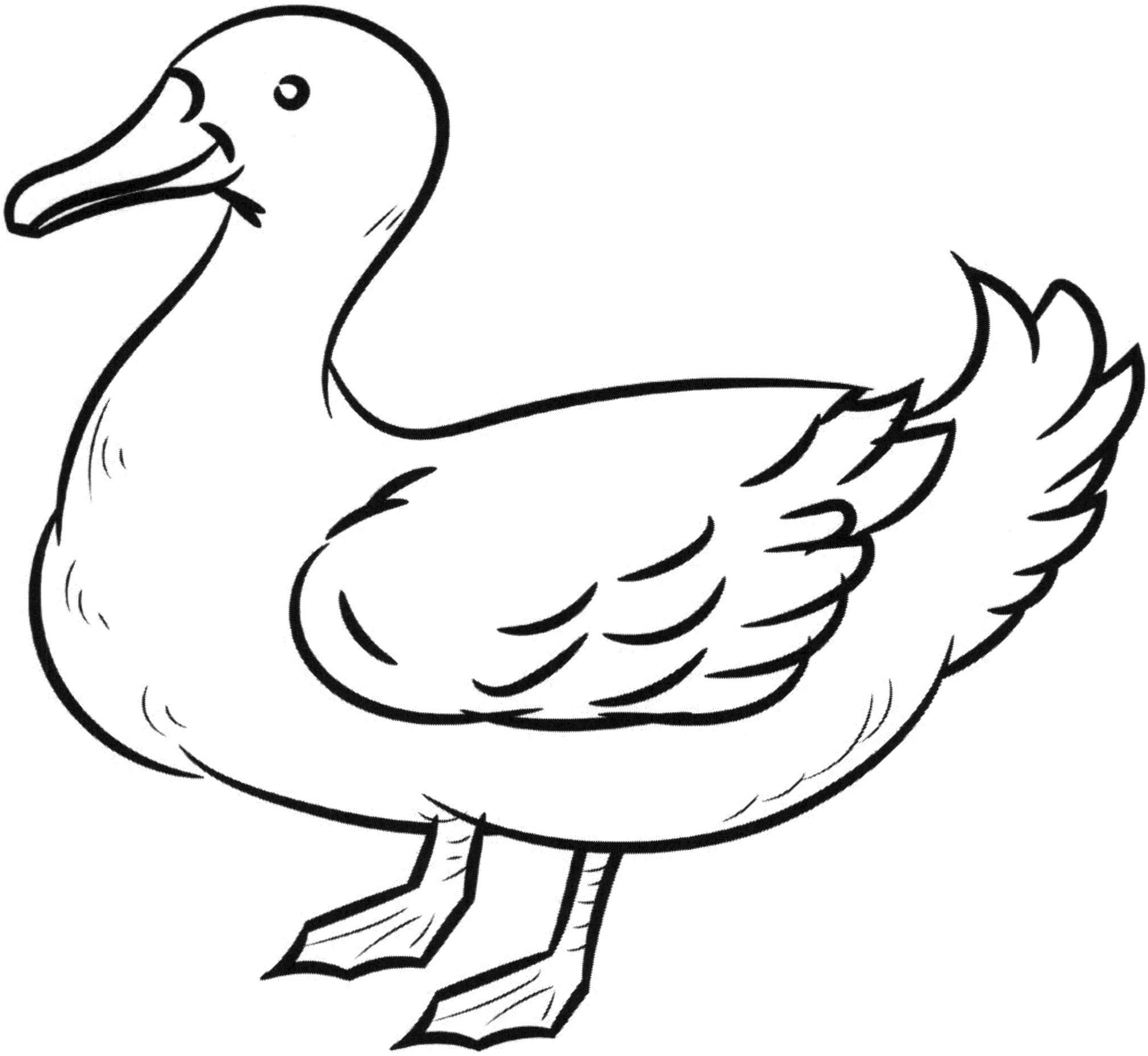

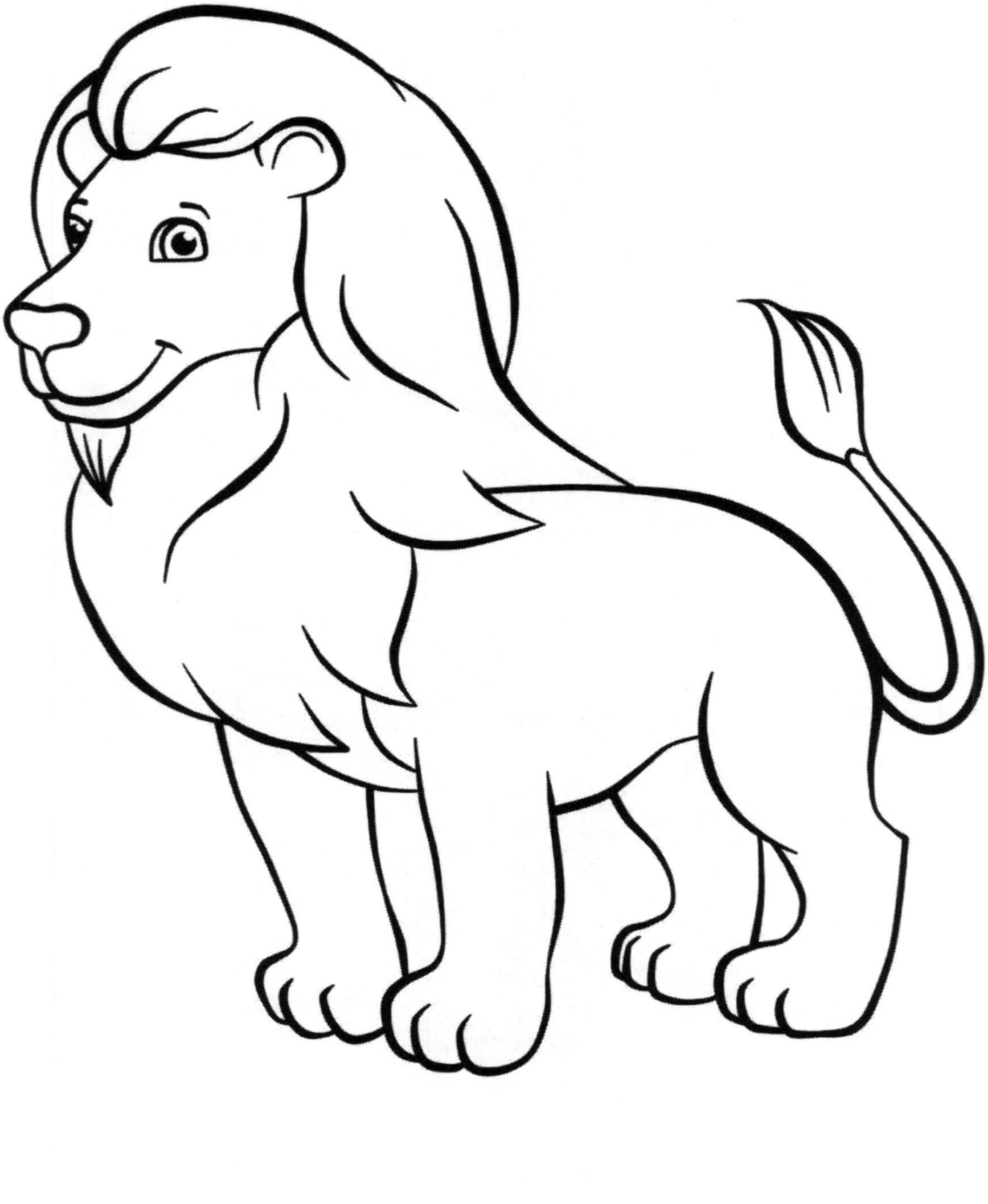

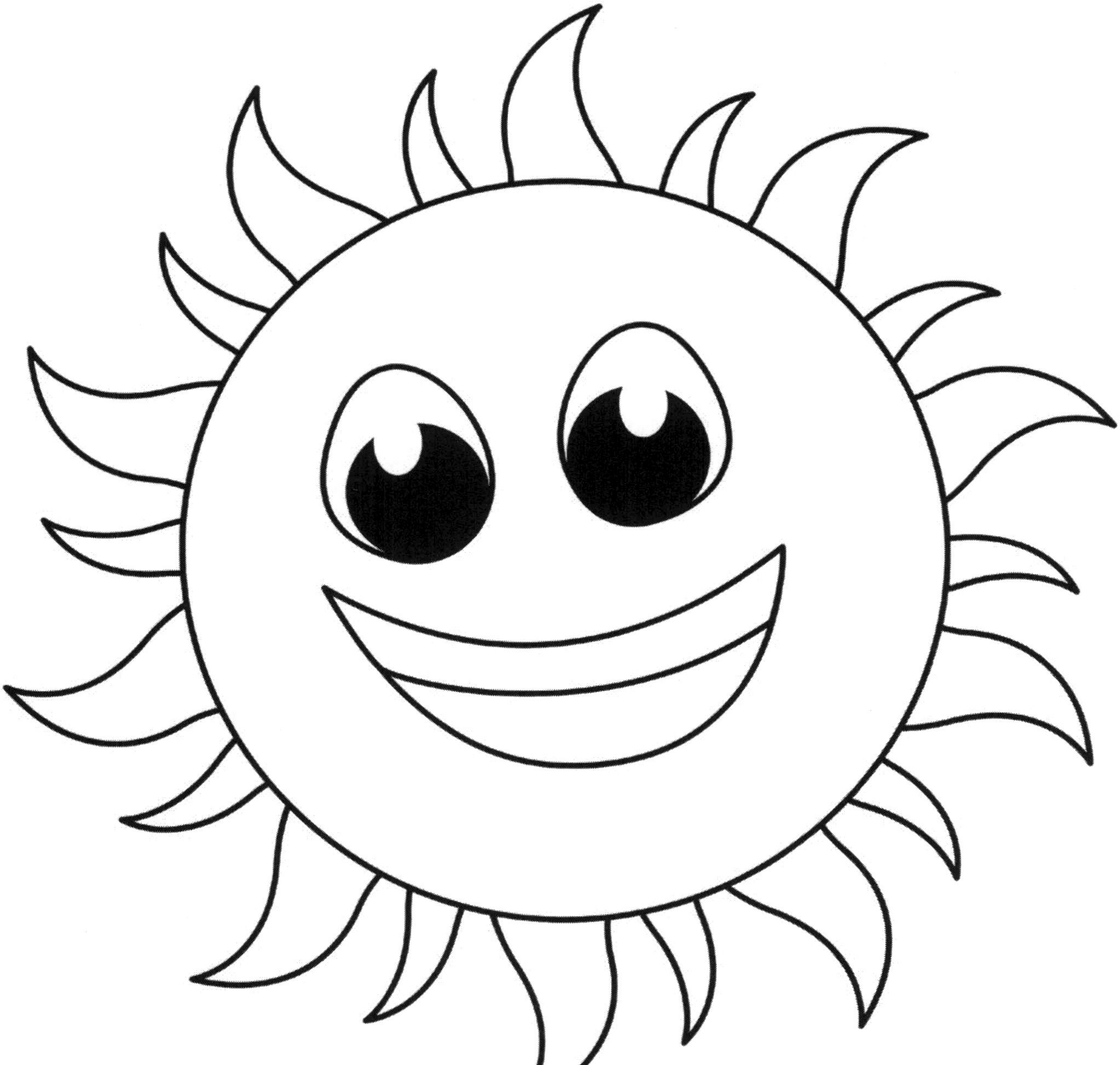

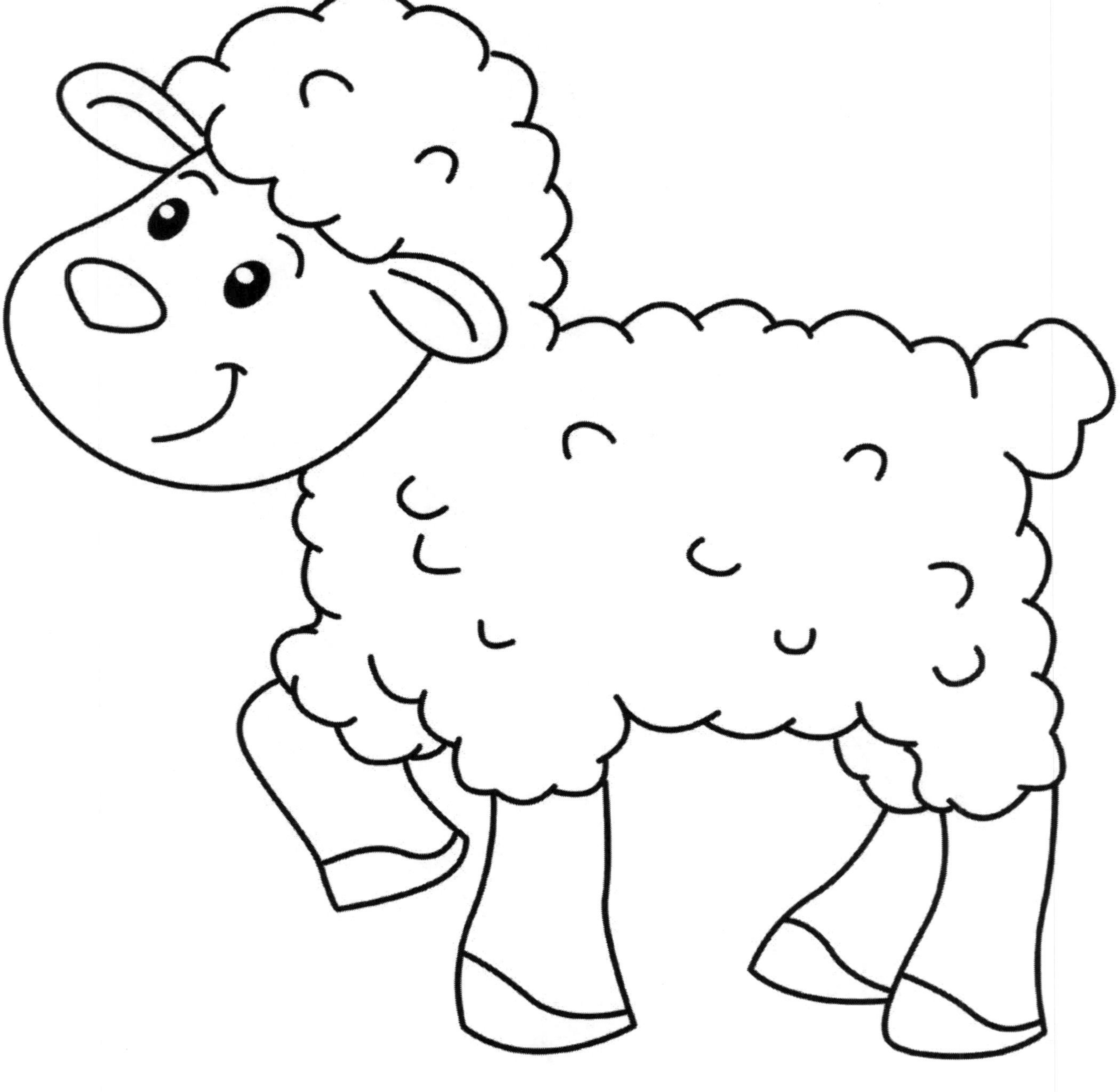

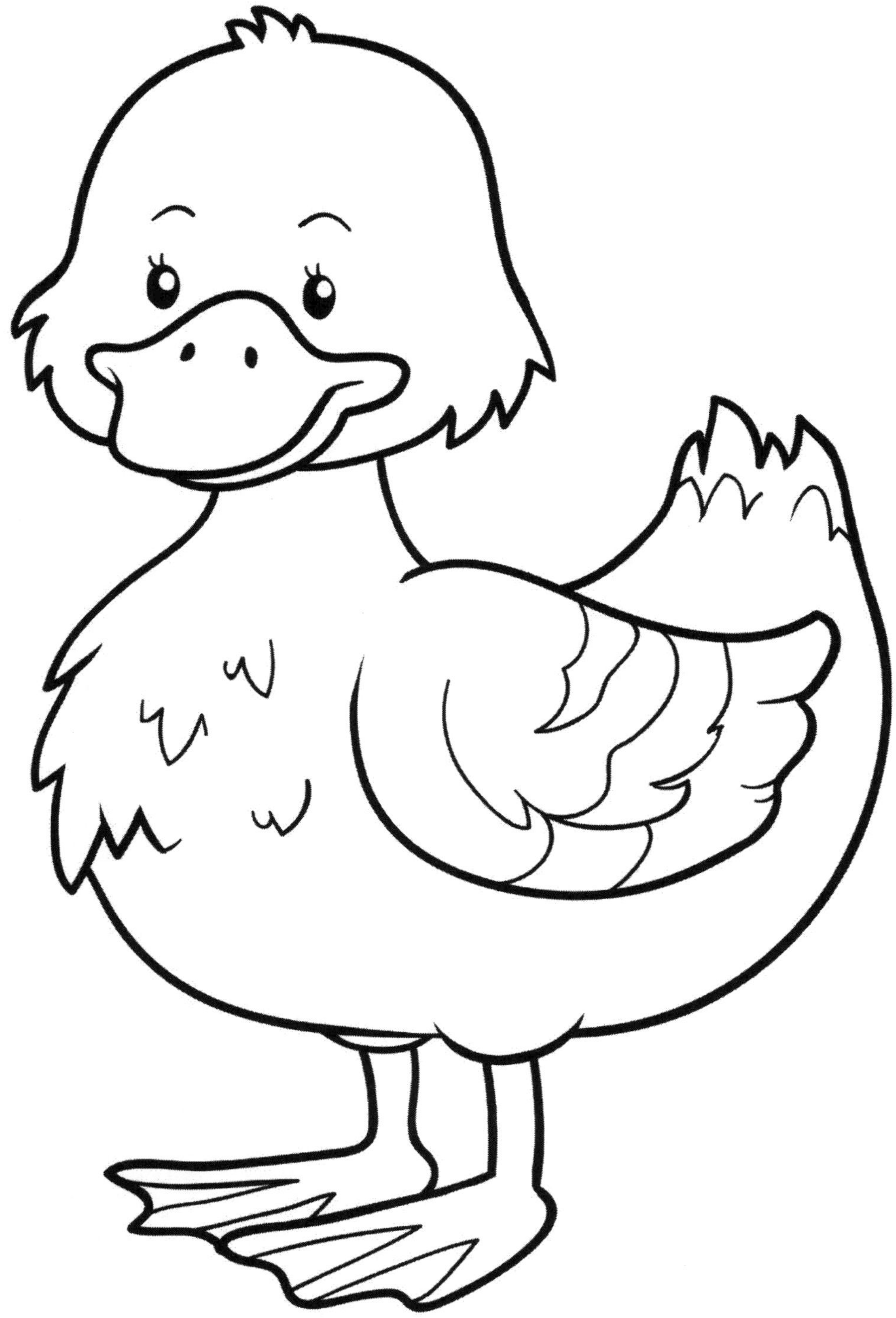

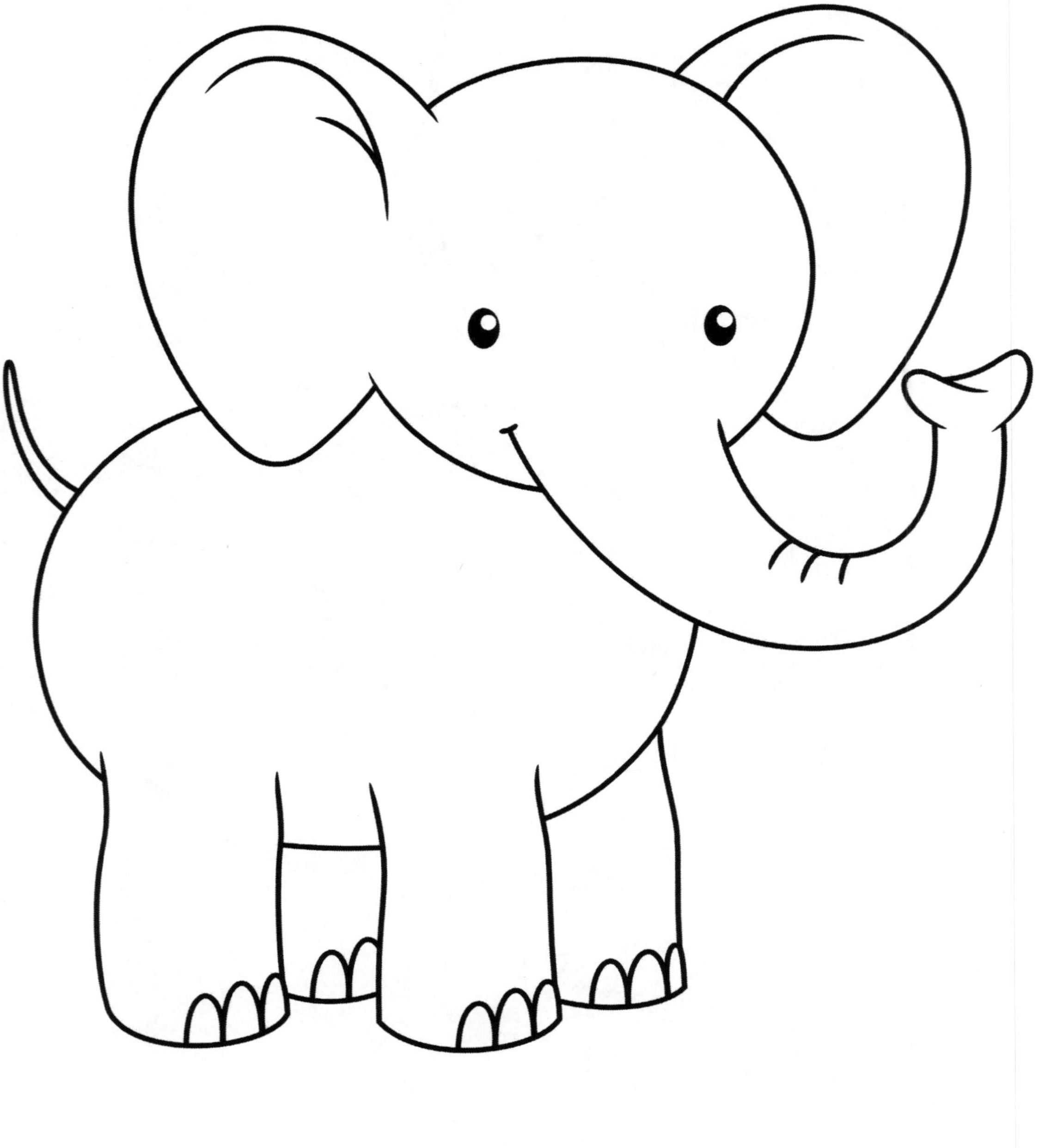

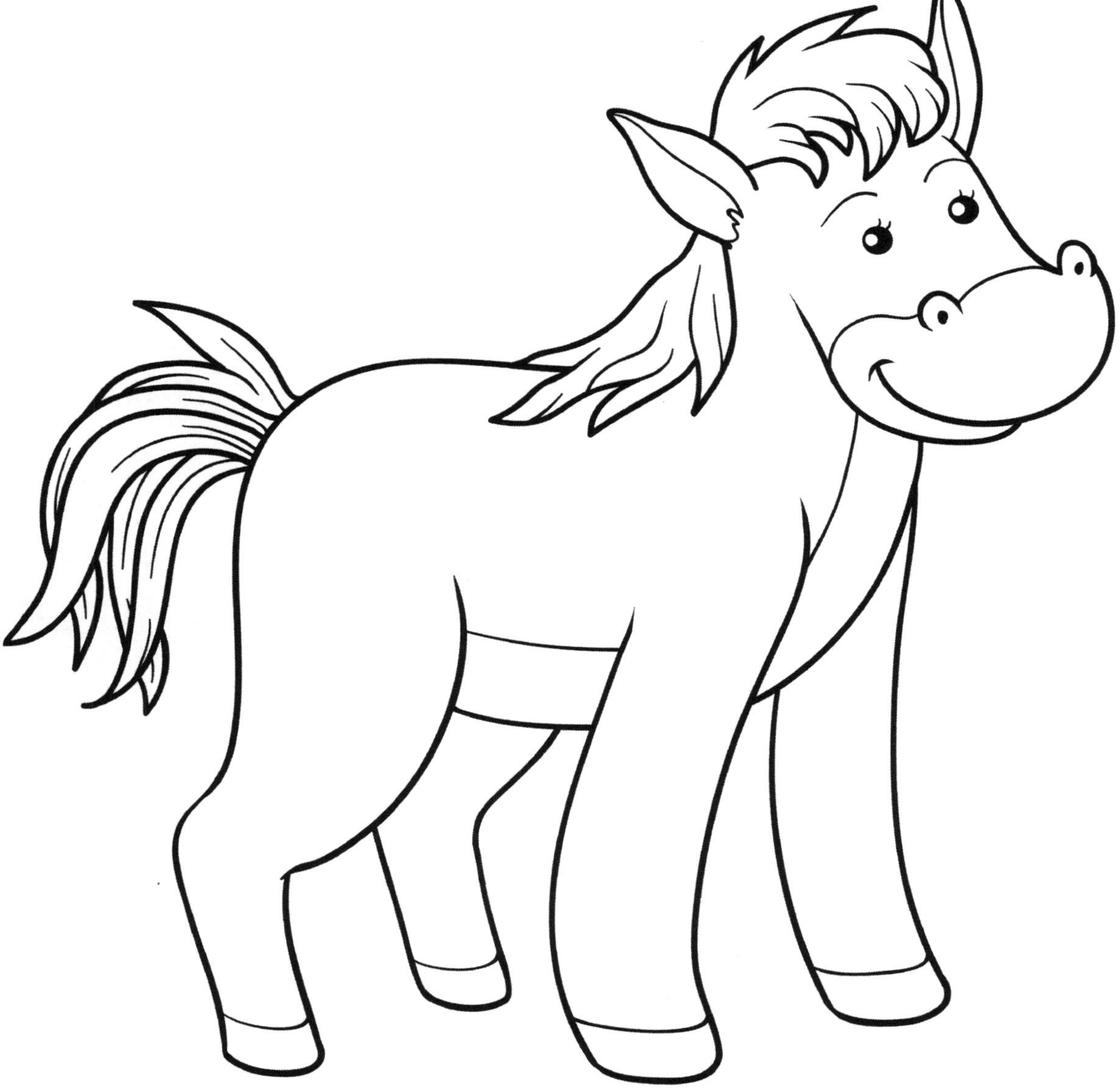

Made in the USA
San Bernardino, CA
04 February 2020

64018704R00031